Family Monographs

Herzfeld

HN
80
.N5
H6

FAMILY MONOGRAPHS

THE HISTORY OF TWENTY-FOUR FAMILIES LIVING
IN THE MIDDLE WEST SIDE OF
NEW YORK CITY

WITH AN INTRODUCTION

By

ELSA G. HERZFELD

Preface by

ELSIE CLEWS PARSONS, Ph. D.
Lecturer on Sociology at Barnard College

NEW YORK
The James Kempster Printing Company
1905

Copyrighted, 1905
BY ELSA G. HERZFELD

Family Monographs

152236

PREFACE.

To Le Play is due the credit of introducing the monograph method as a fruitful means of sociological observation. Neither he nor his many followers in France and elsewhere have ever fully exploited that method, however, particularly in the study of the family. The surprising barrenness of their results is probably to be explained by their undue insistence upon the significance of the economic to the neglect of that of the psychological social fact.

In following the monograph method in the sociological field work at Barnard College greater emphasis has been put upon the non-economic data necessary to an understanding of group psychology, upon the familial, neighborly and institutional interests and activities of the group studied, the family, than upon the purely economic facts relating to the group. In spite of their scientific charm, family budgets and inventories were not as a rule attempted. Accuracy in observing and recording was nevertheless insisted upon[1] and, although the work of the undergraduate student is of necessity primarily pedagogic, the note-book and schedule contributions of the students confirmed their director in her belief in the scientific value

---

[1] Clews: *Field Work in Teaching Sociology*, Educational Review, September, 1900.

of the monograph method and in the advantage of emphasizing the psychological as well as the less valuable although more definite and attractive economic fact.

Miss Herzfeld gave more time and energy to her investigations than the average student. She was likewise an exceptionally competent observer and recorder. It is believed, therefore, that the data of the Family Monographs, however fragmentary and unambitious, may be suggestive to other investigators and helpful to practical people in contact with tenement-house life.

A word or two along both these lines.

The monographs will at once suggest to the ethnologist a comparison of the life of Primitive and Tenement-House Man. Lack of capital, migratory habits,[1] high birth and child-mortality rates, maternal ignorance, uncontrolled parental affection and sense of proprietorship, sex taboos, lack of "self-determination" in matrimonial choice, matrimonial instability, *mutterfolge* (in its literal sense), animistic habits of thought, are circumstances or characters common to both. Whether or not these points of resemblance are due to a common lack of "social surplus" or to other conditions it would be well worth while finding out.

Perhaps the monographs will serve to suggest how little our multitudinous philanthropies touch the real life

---

[1] In the tenement house, as in the primitive family, there even seems to be a tendency to migrate within a given area.

of the tenements. What are the schools, public or parochial, the churches, the settlements, etc., doing to improve home life? Do they teach boys and girls anything about their obligations in marriage and child-rearing? Are not the subjects of conception, pregnancy, confinement and nursing taboo? Does not the institutional life of the boys and girls, of the young men and women, even emphasize through its segregation of the sexes the lack of understanding of one another that particularly characterizes tenement-house people? And is not mutual understanding the basis of comradeship and mutual consideration between the sexes?

ELSIE CLEWS PARSONS.

TABLE OF CONTENTS

Introduction

Object and method of investigation

I

Situation. Table of nationalities represented in families studied. Note on nationalities of neighborhood. Note on assimilation. Mental traits. Reading. Art. Music. "Rackets" and balls. Good and bad luck superstitions. Beliefs and practices about pregnancy, childbirth, lactation. Christening beliefs and practices. Wedding beliefs and practices. Beliefs and practices in regard to deaths and funerals. Attitude towards the church. Attitude towards physicians, hospitals, etc. Attitude towards police department. Political ideas and practices. Relations to neighbors.

II

Table of occupations and wages of members of families studied. Note on membership in trade unions and benefit societies. Note on industries found in the district. Out of work. Family expenditure. A characteristic table of expenditure. Savings. Insurance. A typical apartment. Housekeeping. Habits of moving. Husband and wife. Parents and children. Kinsfolk.

OBJECT AND METHOD OF INVESTIGATION.

The object of these studies is to throw light on the family of the New York tenement-house dweller.

The majority of the families studied are fairly typical of the German and Irish, foreign and native born, tenement-house population of New York. These families are not of the most unfortunate, thriftless type. They live, nevertheless, from hand to mouth. They are frequently on the verge of actual distress, for their wages do not enable them to maintain their physical efficiency. They are often unemployed or work at irregular occupations. In periods of illness want stares them in the face. Nevertheless, they shun "charity." In actual need they first turn to the kinsfolk who are "better off" or they accept the aid of neighbors. The landlord waits, the tradesmen give credit and sometimes the church helps.

As I came to know the twenty-five families described in the monographs more intimately, I became acquainted with their relatives and neighbors. This acquaintance enabled me to get a more general idea of the conditions of the whole neighborhood, a considerable part of the middle West Side of New York city. This general view of the neighborhood I have embodied in part in the introduction.

The investigation was begun in October, 1902, and practically finished by May, 1904.[1]

It must be remembered, however, that my study is not primarily of the neighborhood. Had it been primarily a neighborhood study, a different order would have been followed in the topics of this introduction, and many facts not at present considered or but scantily referred to would have had to be presented at length. In division I certain ethnic facts and facts of the social mind are given. Division II presents facts bearing upon the organization and welfare of the family.[2]

At the outset I became acquainted with the families as a penny provident collector for Hartley House, a social settlement at 415

---

[1] I also had at my disposal the records of the Barnard College students, who, at an earlier date, had visited some of the same families. These records assisted me in correcting inaccuracies, but they did not materially affect my work. [2] Facts about the religious crises of the family are given in Division I in connection with the subject of attitude towards the church.

West Forty-sixth street. Penny provident collecting presents many opportunities for acquiring an intimate knowledge of the families visited. The families may be visited once a week or even oftener, the visits lasting from five minutes to an hour. The relation which springs up between the family and collector is a helpful and natural one. The "bank lady" takes the unwilling mother to the hospital to show her how well the neighbors' children are treated; she speaks of the duty of sending the child to school, of the opportunities offered by the evening schools, playgrounds, recreation centres and settlements. She tries to save her depositors from being exploited by the unscrupulous quack doctor, lawyer, money lender and pawnbroker in the district and by the "pay on the instalment" man in his many disguises. In teaching them to save small sums each week the bright-colored stamp becomes but a fiction for the more effective spending of the family income or the opening of a bank account in a "live" bank. The "bank teacher's" visits become glad occasions. She is invited to the family birthday parties; Christmas and Easter gifts are exchanged. She is sent for when there is sickness or death. She goes to visit the sick child in the hospital. She is expected to go to the wakes and funerals, not only of the members of the family but of the kinsfolk, friends and neighbors. She is taken "to get a last look" at the woman whom she helped to place in the hospital. She attends the weddings, the church fairs and jubilees, and the first communion. She is even asked to "stand for" a child. When a family moves she is required to take a "look" at the new rooms first. When a piano or a new dress is to be purchased, she must help in the selection. The mothers are influenced to employ a family physician. Regular hours of nursing, sleeping and bathing are advocated. Diet is prescribed for young children. Child labor cases are reported to the Child Labor Committee. Better employment is secured for those out of work, for in many cases the unemployed do not know where to go to look for work or whom to ask. Opportunities are given to attend concerts and decent plays. The children are taken to Central Park, Fort Lee and the museums. Sunday excursions are planned.[1]

---
[1] In order to safeguard what are essentially private matters the surnames of the families have been changed. Surnames of the same nationality have been given.

I

SITUATION.

The boundaries of the district under consideration are Fifty-third street on the north, Fortieth street on the south, the North River on the west and Ninth avenue on the east. Most of the families described in the monographs live, however, in Forty-first, Forty-third, Forty-fourth, Forty-fifth and Forty-sixth streets, between Tenth avenue and the river. The thoroughfares are Ninth avenue, Tenth avenue and Eleventh avenue. Over Ninth avenue the elevated railroad runs, below this there is an electric surface car. On Tenth avenue there is another electric surface road, which runs up Broadway at Seventy-second street. There is also a slow and little used horse car. On Eleventh avenue there is a steam railway. Through Forty-second street runs an electric car.

On the avenues and side streets are the usual large number of three and four-story red-brick tenement houses. Each house is occupied by as many families as possible; each family crowds as many people as possible into its few rooms.

The average for the whole 15th Assembly District in which our neighborhood is included is 6.4 families to a house; but as the 15th Assembly District reaches to West Fifty-ninth street,[1] and as the congestion is less farther east, the average number of families for our neighborhood is probably much higher. In the double-deckers in which nineteen out of the twenty-four families of the monographs live there are usually twenty families to a house. There is no way of estimating in all exactly the number of the population in our neighborhood. In 1900 the population of the 15th Assembly District was estimated[2] at 38,911 persons and 9,160 families. In the same year the Tenement-house Department computed the heads of the families in the 22d Ward (West Fortieth street, West Eighty-sixth street, North River to Sixth avenue) at 134,669.

---

[1] 15th Assembly District extends from West Fortieth street to West Fiftieth street, North River to Sixth avenue; our neighborhood West Fifty-third street to West Fortieth street, North River, to Ninth avenue is thus included in the district. [2] "The Distribution of Homes, Churches, Settlements and Saloons in Greater New York," by Rev. W. Laidlaw in *Federation*, March, 1903.

Towards the river the houses, chiefly wooden structures, are more rickety and the factories and stables more numerous. Schools, churches, factories, power houses, dry-goods shops, grocer and butcher stores, bakeries, junk shops, laundries, stables, carpenter shops, delicatessen, cigar, candy and "notion" stores, barber shops, pharmacies and saloons (88) are scattered on the avenues and side streets. Then too, there are attorneys-at-law and doctors' signs, and the ubiquitous midwife announces her presence everywhere.

The streets are always dirty. In winter the unmelted snow is heaped up in the gutters. The pavement is chiefly of cobblestones, the sidewalks are narrow and badly paved. The garbage can and ash barrel standing before the doors are always running over.

TABLE OF NATIONALITY OF PARENTS OF MONOGRAPH FAMILIES.

No. of Monograph.	Descent.		Residence	
	F.	M.	F.	M.
I	English	English	Born in England, 1825; came to N.Y., 1858.	Born in England, 1835; came to N.Y., 1858.
II	Irish	Irish	Born in Ireland, 1832; came to N.Y., 1865.	Born in Ireland, 1859; parents came to N.Y., 1866.
III	Irish	Irish	Born in Ireland, 1832; came to N.Y., 1850.	Born in Ireland, 1835; came to N.Y., 1849.
IV	Irish	Irish	Born in Ireland, 1817, came to N.Y., 1844.	Born in Ireland, 1825; came to N.Y., 1846.
V	Scotch-Dutch	Irish-French	Born in Scotland, 1840; came to N.Y.; 1846.	Born on boat, 1844.
VI	German	German	Born in Germany 1848; came to N.Y., 1886.	Came to N.Y., 1886.
VII	1. German 2. Unknown	French-German	Born in Germany, 1849; came over with parents, 1853. Born in Troy, N.Y., 1850.	Born in N.Y., 1850; father came to N.Y., 1838.
VIII	Irish	Irish	Born in Ireland, 1851, came to Mass., 1876.	Born in Ireland, 1856; came to Mass., 1876.

TABLE OF NATIONALITY OF PARENTS—Continued.

No. of Monograph.	Descent.		Residence.	
	F.	M.	F.	M.
IX	Irish	English	Born in Ireland, 1857.	Born in England, 1871; mother came to N. Y., 1885.
X	German	German	Born in Germany, 1859; came to N.Y., 1880.	Born in Germany, 1864; came to N.Y., 1881.
XI	Welsh-Irish	Irish	Born in Ireland, 1858; mother came to N. Y., 1894.	Born in Ireland, 1875; came to N.Y. previous to 1894.
XII	Irish	Irish	Born in Ireland, 1859; came to N.Y., 1875.	Born in Ireland, came to N.Y. 1880.
XIII	German	German	Born in Germany, 1861; came to N.Y., 1879.	Born in Germany, 1869; came to N.Y., 1884.
XIV	German	German	Born in Germany, 1861; came to N.Y., 1887.	Born in Germany, 1868; came to N.Y., 1885.
XV	Scotch	Irish	Born in Yonkers, 1861, parents came from Scotland, 1855.	Born in N. Y.; mother came from Ireland, 1831.
XVI	German	English-American	Born in Germany, 1852; came to N.Y., 1888.	Born in N.Y., 1870; father came to N.Y., 1830; mother a "Yankee."
XVII	American German	American	Born in Brockport, N.Y., 1853. Born in Yonkers, 1862.	Born in Ohio, 1862.
XVIII	English	French-German	Born in England, 1864; came to N.Y., 1880.	Born in N.Y., 1868; father came to N.Y., 1829, mother, 1840.
XIX	Irish	Irish-American	Born in Ireland, 1864; parents came to N. Y., 1862.	Born in N.Y., 1866.
XX	Irish	Irish	Born in N.Y., 1864; parents came to N. Y., 1860	Born in N.Y., 1862; father came to N.Y., 1850, mother, 1849.
XXI	German	German-English	Born in N.Y., 1866.	Born in N.Y., 1869.
XXII	German	German	Born in N.Y., 1867.	Born in N.Y., 1866.
XXIII	German	Unknown	Born in N.Y., 1871.	Born in N.Y., 1870.
XXIV	Russian Jew	English	Born in N.Y., 1874.	Born in N.Y., 1879.

WARD 22.
TENEMENT HOUSE POPULATION.[1]
Nativity and Parentage of Heads of Families.

Block.	Head of Family.		Parentage.														Color.			Total.
	Native.	Foreign.	U. S.	Aus. Hun.	Bohemia.	France.	Germany	England and Wales.	Ireland.	Italy.	Poland.	Russia.	Scan. and Denmark.	Scotland.	Unknown.	Other Countries.	Mixed.	White.	Black.	Jap., Chin., Indian.	
40th St. bet. 11th and 10th Aves....	73	109	17	2	..	1	69	5	77	1	..	3	2	2	..	..	3	182	..	..	182
40th St. bet. 10th and 9th Aves....	178	261	59	1	..	5	184	11	131	11	1	8	1	5	..	14	8	412	26	1	439
41st St. bet. 12th and 11th Aves....	37	60	13	4	..	2	35	6	30	2	..	1	..	1	..	3	9	96	1	1	97
41st St. bet. 11th and 10th Aves....	129	289	23	5	..	7	160	13	143	26	..	3	7	6	..	16	2	416	1	1	418
41st St. bet. 10th and 9th Aves....	29	34	12	2	..	..	12	2	29	3	..	4	..	3	..	1	2	52	10	1	63
42d St. bet. 12th and 11th Aves....	101	116	21	1	..	4	96	5	117	6	..	3	3	3	..	3	3	267	..	..	267
42d St. bet. 11th and 10th Aves....	74	94	30	2	..	1	33	5	79	3	..	..	2	6	2	3	1	164	4	..	168
42d St. bet. 10th and 9th Aves....	5	13	..	1	..	..	5	1	5	..	..	..	..	..	..	..	..	18	..	..	18
43d St. bet. 12th and 11th Aves....	164	240	84	2	..	3	102	16	187	8	..	3	2	12	..	8	10	387	16	1	404
43d St. bet. 11th and 10th Aves....	123	127	37	1	..	..	67	..	89	3	..	1	6	8	..	..	..	250	..	..	250
44th St. bet. 12th and 11th Aves....	25	30	8	1	..	1	8	1	5	2	..	..	2	..	..	..	8	55	..	..	55
44th St. bet. 11th and 10th Aves....	148	245	74	6	..	3	95	6	34	11	1	5	2	12	2	10	4	337	56	..	393
44th St. bet. 10th and 9th Aves....	168	223	62	1	..	6	141	19	171	7	4	4	2	8	..	14	8	363	28	..	391
45th St. bet. 12th and 11th Aves....	22	35	5	..	..	1	25	3	21	5	..	..	..	..	..	4	1	57	..	..	57
45th St. bet. 11th and 10th Aves....	118	263	23	5	..	5	110	9	121	11	..	..	4	6	..	17	12	381	..	..	381
45th St. bet. 10th and 9th Aves....	147	253	48	2	1	2	115	15	139	38	1	..	4	6	..	2	9	399	1	..	400
46th St. bet. 12th and 11th Aves....	60	88	16	4	..	..	35	3	73	11	..	..	..	6	..	6	10	148	..	..	148
46th St. bet. 11th and 10th Aves....	152	276	28	4	..	7	167	9	173	30	4	4	9	10	..	6	10	428	..	..	428
46th St. bet. 10th and 9th Aves....	236	337	92	4	..	1	150	..	209	..	..	4	..	11	2	6	11	562	10	1	573
47th St. bet. 12th and 11th Aves....	36	58	6	2	4	1	48	6	29	9	2	2	2	5	..	7	11	335	..	..	335
47th St. bet. 11th and 10th Aves....	116	219	16	1	2	1	142	2	126	1	3	2	..	11	..	7	12	454	..	..	454
47th St. bet. 10th and 9th Aves....	194	260	56	7	1	4	143	4	188	11	4	..	10	5	..	1	10	94	..	..	94
48th St. bet. 12th and 11th Aves....	21	84	4	1	..	3	35	4	21	31	..	2	..	..	..	7	11	105	..	..	105
48th St. bet. 11th and 10th Aves....	194	414	42	5	2	5	193	13	281	11	1	2	8	9	2	17	16	608	..	..	608
48th St. bet. 10th and 9th Aves....	273	422	75	4	1	8	221	26	296	5	..	1	10	14	..	21	12	683	12	..	695
49th St. bet. 12th and 11th Aves....	3	6	4	..	..	..	1	..	7	..	..	..	..	..	..	..	..	9	..	..	9
49th St. bet. 11th and 10th Aves....	181	347	64	4	5	2	137	12	246	12	1	5	4	5	3	13	15	481	47	..	528
49th St. bet. 10th and 9th Aves....	191	260	48	2	..	4	179	16	174	7	..	..	2	8	..	7	3	451	..	..	451
50th St. bet. 12th and 11th Aves....	5	..	..	..	..	..	..	..	4	..	..	1	..	..	..	..	..	5	..	..	5
50th St. bet. 11th and 10th Aves....	201	285	43	2	..	3	169	17	202	4	..	1	5	13	2	12	13	483	3	..	483

FAMILY MONOGRAPHS

WARD 22—Continued.
TENEMENT HOUSE POPULATION.
Nativity and Parentage of Heads of Families.

Block.	Head of Family.		Parentage.															Color.			Total.
	Native.	Foreign.	U.S.	Aus. Hun.	Bohemia.	France.	Germany.	England and Wales.	Ireland.	Italy.	Poland.	Russia.	Scan. and Denmark.	Scotland.	Unknown.	Other Countries.	Mixed.	White.	Black.	Jap., Chin., Indian.	
50th St. bet. 10th and 9th Aves....	193	269	44	5	..	7	164	22	169	5	..	1	4	12	1	10	18	462	..	..	462
51st St. bet. 12th and 11th Aves....	32	61	6	..	..	..	34	3	36	3	..	2	1	4	..	4	..	93	..	..	93
51st St. bet. 11th and 10th Aves....	130	205	26	1	..	1	124	8	128	3	..	6	5	6	1	13	12	335	..	..	335
51st St. bet. 10th and 9th Aves....	165	225	92	..	..	1	69	11	194	8	..	3	3	8	..	4	2	331	59	..	390
53d St. bet. 12th and 10th Aves....	190	355	103	4	1	2	109	10	259	4	..	5	6	13	..	12	15	545	..	..	545
53d St. bet. 10th and 9th Aves....	192	494	60	5	..	3	149	12	401	18	2	6	11	3	..	10	8	685	..	1	686
53d St. bet. 12th and 10th Aves....	59	91	9	1	..	..	87	3	36	1	..	1	4	3	..	3	4	150	..	..	150
53d St. bet. 10th and 9th Aves....	12	8	7	..	..	..	4	1	6	..	..	..	..	..	..	..	1	19	1	..	20

[1] From page 92—Compiled from tables of first Report of the Tenement-house Department of the City of New York, 1902-1903. Number living between W. 53d and W. 40th Sts. from 12th to 9th Avenues, 11,112. Total population living in 22d Ward, 134,669.

NOTES ON ASSIMILATION.

Often the Irish do not wish to be called Irish because that implies a term of contempt. When asked why the name has come to be of such evil repute, the Irishman will tell you that he attributes it chiefly to the drinking habits and "unscrupulessness" of certain politicians who masquerade as Irishmen. Nevertheless the Irishman never ceases to sentimentalize about the hills and valleys of the "ould country." He looks forward to going home some day on a visit when he has "saved up enough!"[1] The Irish are particularly attached to the country or district they come from. One woman knew some friends who had "gone back" to attend the dedication of a cathedral in their country.[2] She received the newspaper from Ireland describing the important event.

The German emigrant likes to speak his native language. Frequently he does not learn to read English, knowing that he can buy the *Staatszeitung* at the news-stand.[3] His American-born children protest against studying the language and refuse to speak it! They would rather learn French. If the parents go to a church in which the services are in German the children go to another church.[4]

The German-American child wants a position in an office.[5] The daughter refuses to go into domestic service although her mother had formerly taken a "position." She has learned to play the piano and wants to be a "lady."

The German and American element have a distinct contempt for the Irish as a class. The Irish are always low, coarse and vulgar or they are "dirty" and "do not even know their own ages!" "They drink and fight continually." One woman did not wish to send her children to a certain public school in the neighborhood, because there were "so many Micks going there."[6]

When there is a German-Irish quarrel in a house the Irish family below comes up to help. The German and American children frequently bully the "Irish kid." The German ridicules the Irishman's brogue, his "for shur" and "speeck," etc. The

---

[1] Monograph ii. [2] Monograph viii. [3] Monograph x. [4] Monograph xxi. [5] Monograph x.
[6] Monograph ii.

Irishman sometimes refers to his German neighbors as those "awful Dutch."

I met with instances of ill-feeling between Irish and English families. One Irish woman, whose husband was an Englishman, railed against all English people.[1] She took for granted that all Englishmen beat their wives because at times her husband beat her. The Irish are tolerant save towards the Scotch-Irish. "They spoil the chance of all of us Irish in America."[2]

The German and Irish both will tell you that the Italian is "spoiling the neighborhood." The German says that he comes in contact with the "dagos" in the iron industries in which the Italian and Jew are taking his place. "The Italian takes all the money he earns out of the country. His groceries are not as fresh as ours and if you buy coal from him he will cheat you."

A "sheenie" is a landlord or someone "who is very black" or "a boy what don't eat pork."

All the nationalities feel antipathy towards the negro. They call them thieves, "dirty pigs," etc., and refuse to live in the same house with them or sit next them in school. One house in West Forty-fifth street is known as "the nigger place."

MENTAL TRAITS.

Even those of the members of the family who have had a fairly good amount of schooling possess small reasoning powers. They show some small curiosity, but it is rather that of a child, than the intellectual desire to know. They lose patience when they are unable to comprehend a thing in the beginning. The questions they ask are frequently childish ones. They think there is something wrong with you if you do not believe in the efficacy of dreams, the fate prophesied to you by the fortune teller, the healing power of things blessed by the priest, etc. They never argue; they are seldom persuaded that their course of action has been wrong.

READING.

The *Little Morning News, New York Journal, The World, Evening Telegram, The Press* and *The Herald* are read either

---

[1] Monograph xviii. [2] Monograph iv.

in the morning or evening or, sometimes, at both times. The *Staatszeitung* is also read by the German families. The husband reads early in the morning or at night, sometimes he spends his Sunday reading the papers![1] One man kept his papers for months and months and read them over and over. He persisted in saying that "the old ones is better than the new." A few of the women buy their own papers, if they have no other opportunities of seeing a paper.[2] The latest murder, the war news, the last automobile accident, the fashionable wedding, the description of the gowns the box-holders wore at the opera, etc., form the chief topic of conversation between neighbor and neighbor. The women themselves have little opportunity to read. When they do read at all, their literature is always of a most sensational and sentimental nature. The children of school age are frequently glad of an opportunity to get books from the public school, church or settlement library.[3] There is very little reading matter for children under school age. Sometimes a family[4] possesses a few books. Among them are books of conundrums, jokes, "magic," "parlor tricks," and "fortune telling." Every family has its bible with a registry of births and deaths in the family. They keep the marriage licenses and baptismal certificates in the drawer of a bureau. The families buy "penny family papers." These are passed from tenant to tenant and read with great eagerness.[5] They consist usually of thrilling tales of adventure, love stories, detective stories, mining episodes, etc.

ART.

"Everybody" has crayons and chromos of grandparents, aunts, uncles, brothers, sisters, brothers' wives, sisters' husbands, etc. These are copied from photographs or are original productions of "an artist," who "comes 'round" and is paid on the instalment plan. The crayon is also paid for in coupons given by the family grocer.[6] It may also be "given free" when a dozen pictures have been ordered.[7] One woman whose husband's family did not figure in her portrait gallery said she "felt awfully ashamed because you might think my husband had no folks."[8]

---

[1] Monograph ii.   [2] Monographs iv, v.   [3] Monographs v, x, xxiii.   [4] Monograph x.
[5] Monograph ii.   [6] Monograph xviii.   [7] Monograph xxi.   [8] Monograph xxiii.

There are many pictures of animals, sunsets, moonlight landscapes, mountains and rivers. These pictures are wedding presents or have been "picked up at a sale" or "bought on the avenue or from a peddler," or acquired with cigar coupons or given gratis by a Sunday paper. "The Haunted Castle," "In the Country," "By the River," "A Mowing," Millet's "The Angelus," "The Mill," etc. Sentimental or heroic subjects are popular— "Our Baby," "Mama's Pet," an allegorical representation of "Motherhood," "At Twilight," "Comin' Thro' the Rye," "Lovelorn Maid," "The First Proposal," to the more dramatic representations of "The Wreck," "Romeo and Juliet," and the "Moor and Desdemona."

In the Irish Catholic home the colored religious print is always found. "The Infant Jesus," "The Mother and the Child," "The Childhood of Saint Bernard," "Saint Anthony's Temptation" (a copy of the famous original) are placed on the wall. I found few copies of great paintings, except a few more modern, as Hoffman's "Christ in the Garden of Gethsemene," Bougereau's "Pietà." In every Catholic home there are crucifixes either of light wood, black ebony, enameled or white glass. There are frequently china figures representing the Virgin Mary and the Christ child, colored in bright reds and blues with golden halos.

There were many soap coupon pictures of Abraham Lincoln, George Washington, William McKinley and one of "Liberty." Some of these had home-made frames of colored and gilt paper and ribbon. One family had all their pictures framed in tobacco box wood with the yellow ribbons for "fasteners."[1]

The mantels are always adorned with cheap china vases and tin ornaments. I found two instances in which the family had invested in the plaster statuary the "dago" on the street peddled. One of these, a Diana, had been gilded, together with all the other ornaments in the parlor, to make them look "fine." The other cast, a Venus, had been draped in purple ribbon to match the "tidy" on the table. When I asked the reason for this her owner said she objected to the "naked woman." "It wasn't a bit polite to her visitors to have that kind of thing around."[2]

[1] Monograph iv. [2] Monograph xvii.

I found few examples at original decoration. One was that of a small boy who drew for me a Christmas gift, a battle between the Russians and Japanese, which he had copied from the paper.[1] He spent much of his time drawing "Buster Brown" and the "Yaller Kid." Another case was that of a small girl, who drew in chalk on the green kitchen wall "The House my Aunt is Going to Live in When She Gets a Feller."[2] One young woman put the weaving mats and sewing cards of her small brother on the kitchen wall.[3] A marble polisher, I knew, carved a large crucifix and a pyramidal watch charm out of a piece of marble the "boss" had discarded.[4] In several families[5] I found proverbs embroidered in cross stitch on canvas and framed. The quotations were either religious or referred to the home. In one German home[6] these were especially elaborate. This home also had pictures of Beethoven, Wagner, Schiller and Goethe at Weimar, which had been brought over by the family.

There are a few small and poorly equipped flower shops in the district. These are patronized chiefly for wreathes which are most frequently made of straw, wax or other artificial flowers. I found one stationery store which fills orders for "memory cards" elaborately edged in gilt with pictures of angels above. The card expresses the sorrow of the family and gives the dates of birth and death of the deceased (dates of confirmation and communion are sometimes added). Below these is a quotation from the bible. They are sent to friends by the family of the deceased.

I also found in the homes several instances of wax wreathes, ornamented with silver and framed in glass and wood.[7] In one case the photograph of the dead father with the date of birth, death and marriage, names of wife, children, etc., were inscribed in gold lettering, a variation probably of the "memory card." One woman[8] had a photograph of the tombstone she had erected in Ireland in memory of her father. She showed it with great pride.

MUSIC.

In several instances the grown daughter took piano lessons.

[1] Monograph xviii. [2] Monograph xvii. [3] Monograph v. [4] Monograph ii.
[5] Monographs ii, iv, xvi, xxi. [6] Monograph xvi. [7] Monographs ii, xvii.
[8] Monograph viii.

The lessons were given in the evening twice a week, costing from fifty cents to a dollar. The teacher guarantees perfect playing "within the year." "Pieces" are given from the beginning. One girl took lessons at Hartley House at ten cents a lesson and practiced at her aunt's "up-town."[1] In one family the girl played so "fine" that the family "hired" a piano.[2] Later on they decided to buy it. They paid each month on the instalment plan until the hundred dollars had been paid. One woman took lessons from an Italian violin artist during her childhood.[3] Later she studied music in Frankfort. She is fairly familiar with classical music and has a natural love for the best. In order to have "pin money" (in reality to keep her from starving) she played the obligatoes at several church concerts. At one time she had to pawn her violin for six dollars a month. She begged the pawnbroker to give it to her the night she played in the church concert because the one the priest had offered her was "so bad." Several women attended Sunday evening services in order to sing.[4] The Catholics spoke with pride of their fine choir. Several of the children went to singing class at Hartley House.[5] Outside of the simple hymns the songs are of a very low order—printed in the newspaper supplement or penny magazine. "The Red Rose and the White," "The Lost Love," "Sweet Kitty," "You and I," are specimens. Occasionally the children sing at home the songs they learn in kindergarten.[6] The German parents know the German folk songs. They have a natural love for music and song. The Irish like the music of the organ grinder and the street singer or the loud shrieking in the music halls. They all sing "coon songs."

"RACKETS" AND BALLS.

Your "gentleman friend" invites you to a "racket" or ball. The former differs from the latter in that refreshments are served free. There is a "show" beforehand, consisting of singing, dancing, "tricks and the like." The "racket" is "run off" by a number of young men or by a club. The usual object is to make money. Almost any one may buy a ticket. If the racket is to be a large one you must expect "a mixed crowd." The usual price of the

---

[1] Monograph xiii. [2] Monograph xvii. [3] Monograph xvi. [4] Monographs x, xiv, xxi. [5] Monographs viii, xiii, xix, xxiii. [6] Monograph x.

ticket is fifty cents.[1] As a usual thing this does not include "wardrobe." This admits gentleman and lady. The coat checks are extra. Ladies ten cents, gentlemen a quarter. They are sold at the door and handed to the woman up stairs in the dressing-rooms. If you buy a ticket from a friend who is not "running off the racket with you" he will ask you to take "a come back" when his racket "comes off." If one club buys the tickets of another club, it sends representatives and throws its "comp." to advertise its next racket. If the club gives the tickets away it can not honorably give away "comps." at that affair. The different clubs vie with one another to get the opening night of "opening date" for their racket or picnic.

A dance is either a "plain affair" or a masquerade. You wear, if possible, a new dress.[2] Sometimes the prettiest girl gets a prize. The gentlemen "club in" to buy these. Your "gentleman friend" dances with you mostly, but he can ask your "lady friend." There is little introducing. The music is "furnished by the professor and his band." Sometimes only a few musicians are "hired." It is not customary to "sit out a dance." This would be equivalent to an "understanding." Taking a girl " 'round the waist" is not thought of as a serious thing. "Spieling" is the order of the evening. The young men stand at one end of the hall and the girls stay together at the other. When two girls attempt to dance together the young men run to separate them. On a Saturday night the party keeps up till four A. M., but if it is on a "week night" it rarely lasts longer than two or three o'clock.

GOOD AND BAD LUCK SUPERSTITIONS, ETC.

Amulets are worn for good luck. A scapula wards off disease.[3] A heart worn as a charm will bring a sweetheart.[4] Books of magic "speak true." Dreams are prophetic, they foretell sorrow, joy and the arrival of letters.[5,6] Fortunes may be determined by tea leaves.[7] It is unsafe to go out by another door than the one by which you enter a room.[8] If a dog howls bad luck "is sure to

---

[1] If the man goes alone the ticket is sold for thirty-five cents. A single girl pays only fifteen cents. [2] Monograph ii, vii, xvii. [3] Monograph ii. [4] Monograph xviii. [5, 6] Monographs ii, xiv. [7] Monograph xviii. [8] Monographs x, xvii.

come before sundown."[1] It is unlucky to comb your hair after dark.[2] Never attempt anything new on Friday.[3] Peacock feathers have an evil influence. Relics of the Saints, of the Cross and mantles worn by them, all have healing power.[4,5] The grandmother of a child whose right side was paralyzed[6] took her to the Church of John the Baptist (Seventy-sixth street, between Third and Lexington avenues), she laid her in the pew, the priest placed the relics of Saint Anne on her as she slept, then he prayed. When she awoke she was cured. She walked to the elevated station. Saint Anne had heard the prayer and the child prays to Anne daily.

BELIEFS AND PRACTICES ABOUT PREGNANCY, CHILDBIRTH, LACTATION, ETC.

Although "it is God's will and not man's that the child comes to us,"[7] frequently the women prolong the lactation period to avoid conception. All the mothers complain that they have to bear too many children. One mother[8] believed that the parent who "wished hardest" could control the sex of the unborn child. "Some women have no luck with boys."[9]

A pregnant woman must avoid all fright or the child will die. If the mother is frightened by injuries received by her husband, the child will be born with the same flaw.[10] It is unlucky to be born with a birthmark. A pregnant woman must never catch her breath nor cross her hands over her heart or the child will be born with heart trouble. A woman in "the family way" must never go to a funeral or the child is sure to die.[11] Great importance is placed in the desire a pregnant woman may have to eat a certain thing. The child will never want to eat that article of food.[12] A pregnant woman is supposed to abstain from certain foods before delivery. After the child is born she may not eat meat lest the child should suffer. One woman stole meat from the supper table and ate it. She says it made the "baby sick."[13] "A child born in May is always lucky."[14] "The Sunday child

---

1 Monograph iii.   2 Monograph iii.   3 Monograph xv.   4, 5 Monographs ii, vii.
6 Monograph ii.   7 Monographs ii, viii, xiv.   8 Monograph xviii.   9 Monograph xv.
10 Monograph ii.   11 Monograph xvii.   12 Monograph xviii.   13 Monograph xviii.
14 Monograph ix.

(Sonntagskind) is born with gold in its pocket."[1] When a child comes "right after a dead one, the child may be still-born."[2] Only the female sex may be present at birth. The women prefer having a midwife to a physician because they are "ashamed."[3]

The period of nursing varies with the nationality, but a child must not be nursed for a period of more than three years, otherwise it will "grow up to be stupid."[4] A child that is weaned on Good Friday "forgets quickest."[5] A child once weaned must never be nursed again or "bad luck" will follow it.[6] If a child is born with teeth it will surely turn out to be a murderer.[7] It is unlucky to rub babies gums.[8] If you do it, the child will have a sharp temper.[9,10] A mother's milk is used to transmit health and strength. One child had sore eyes,[11] they were washed with the mother's milk. "The eyes were well again in a few days." Infant's finger-nails must be torn or bitten off, otherwise the child will be a thief.[12] If you pass a baby through a window, "it will become a thief." The person who discovers a child's first tooth must make it a gift.[13] If a baby looks in the glass while teething it makes the teeth harder to cut. If there are two boys and two girls in a family both boys will not grow up.[14]

CHRISTENING BELIEFS AND PRACTICES.

The mother and child are unclean until they are churched. It is only after the holy water has been applied that the uncleanliness is removed. In Catholic families the child is christened before the end of the first week, until then "it is not safe from harm."[15] An unbaptised child will die much more easily.[16] In the case of the approaching death of an unbaptised child, any one present may rescue it from the evil one.[17] It is unlucky to give the child a name before christening. Frequently the son is named for the father, but the mother does not "like" to give her name to the female child. The child is not to be named after a dead relative,[18] otherwise it is sure to die.[19] If an additional name is given it is to "give the child good luck.[20]

---

1 Monograph x.   2 Monograph ii.   3 She also sent for a powder to cure the drink habit. She put it in her husband's food but he found it out.   4 Monograph xviii.   5 Monograph xviii.   6 Monograph ii.   7 Monograph viii.   8 Monograph xv.   9, 10 Monographs vii. xiv.   11 Monograph vii.   12 Monographs xiv, xvii.   13 Monographs x, xiv.   14 Monograph viii.   15 Monograph ii.   16 Monograph x.   17 Monographs ii, viii.   18 Monographs i, viii, xx.   19 Monographs i, viii, xx.   20 Monographs iv, viii, xviii.

The invitation to "stand for a child" is regarded as an honor which it is unlucky to refuse. The mother thinks her child will grow to be like its godparents.[1] It is unlucky for the child if its godparents die.[2] The godmother must wear clean clothes to church or the child will be "dirty."[3] Frequently the child must have a new dress, but the christening robe may be worn by all the children in the family and become a heirloom.[4] It is unlucky to borrow a christening robe.[5]

Before going to church the child ought to be carried through the house to protect it from disease.[6] A child must be taken to church "on a straight line" or it will lose its way in later life.[7] A child on the way to church must not meet a funeral. It will die if it does. If it does not cry during the performance of the sacrament it will never grow up.[8] The name given the child[9] is a symbol of its new life. The godmother and friends congratulate the parents because the child is a "Christian."[10]

WEDDING BELIEFS AND PRACTICES.

Fortunate is the bride whom the sun shines upon. A girl must not "stand for" a bride more than three times or she will never be married.[11] If the rice is thrown on any but the bride, ill-luck is sure to come.[12] Misfortune is sure to come if you sell or pawn a wedding gift.[13] Above all, never "hock" your wedding ring.[14] Be sure to keep it on the finger a long time if you want to be happy. If you work on the day of your wedding you will have to work always.[15]

BELIEFS AND PRACTICES IN REGARD TO DEATH AND FUNERALS.

No cooking is done in the house of death. No one must touch a *crepe* on the door of a house in which death has occurred. It is "God's sin" to do so. One day I came upon a small boy on a doorstep, crying bitterly. His friend said that he was sure he was going to die. Through curiosity he had touched some of the wax flowers and *crepe* at the door of a dead neighbor. His playfellows had said "God will damn you."

---

[1] Monograph xiv. Where special emphasis was laid on spiritual bond existing between child and godmother. [2] Monograph xvi. [3] Monograph x. [4] Monograph ii. [5] Monograph x. [6] Monograph v. [7] Monograph xvii. [8] Monograph xvii. [9] Monograph x. [10] Monograph xiv. [11] Monograph vii. [12] Monograph xviii. [13] Monograph vii. [14] Monograph xviii. [15] Monographs xvii, xviii.

The Irish fear that wearing green will cause death.[1] One girl bought green material for a dress.[2] It was "made up." Soon after she and her brother were "seized with a fever." Her brother died and she was sick for a long time. It is unlucky to wear the clothes of a deceased person.[3] The family must avoid moving to rooms in which death has occurred, otherwise there will be more deaths.[4] There are certain houses where "people just die off" (this has nothing to do with unsanitary conditions).[5] When a young child dies, it is best not to mourn, because it is better off in Heaven, or because it is an angel. An unbaptised[6] child is mourned because it is not buried in consecrated ground.[7]

The warnings of approaching death are many. The belief in the Banshee is widespread among the Irish residents. One family[8] represented her as a woman in a trailing white dress who hovers about the precincts and wails loudly when death is approaching. She is a good woman, but she foretells death. The Banshee never comes to America. She is afraid to cross the ocean, but there are plenty of ghosts and spirits in New York without her. Monograph iv also relates that in County Cavan, Ireland, "a nice girl" is not buried without "salie rods" (sticks of the salie tree are peeled, decorated with white ribbons and stuck in the newly-made grave as a symbol of purity). In one of the lakes of Cavan[9] there is a "round castle with a round tower." This castle became drowned when its lord was defending it from the invading Danes. "The water came up" and "it sank into the lake." "At times you can see the tower." Blessed is he who is buried on a rainy day. When a certain child was about to die[10] his mother heard a noise as if "the devil himself were falling down stairs." The same woman is not afraid of ghosts. "There is only one Ghost, the Holy Ghost, and he wont follow you if you behave yourself. The Devil is too busy somewhere else."

It is possible "for a dead person to wish some one away."[11] Ghosts are quite likely to deceive persons by deceptive allurements. If the vision comes as a "Sister" it is the "Lord's will"[12] that a thing is to happen.

---

[1] Monograph iv.   [2] Monograph v.   [3] Monograph xviii.   [4] Monograph iv.
[5] Monographs xii, xv.   [6] Monograph iv.   [7] Monograph ii.   [8] Monograph iv.
[9] Monograph iv.   [10] Monograph xviii.   [11] Monograph xv.   [12] Monographs ii, xix.

If you do not attend your neighbor's wake you are likely to have no mourners at your own. If there are not plenty of coaches, a fine casket and an elaborate display of flowers, your neighbors will say "you do not mean well by the dead." You must wear mourning clothes out of respect for the dead.[1] Mrs. Green says she "would rather any day go to a funeral than a wedding."

In many cases not only all the "insurance money" is used up, but large sums are borrowed in order to have a big funeral. Frequently the family pays for the coaches used by the neighbors.

ATTITUDE TOWARDS THE CHURCH.

Many of the residents who are church members do not attend regularly; "nobody cares now if we go or not"[2] they say. "What's the use of going to church if you don't know the people as comes there," or "or don't know how long you will stay in the neighborhood."[3] The mother has no one to care for her children, so she must stay at home at "church time." The mother who can not go on Sunday, sometimes makes an effort to go on high church holidays or at times of joy or sorrow.

The men go to church even less than the women. Occasionally, they have to work on Sundays;[4] at other times, they prefer to sit at home to read the news and smoke. One man,[5] a German, stayed at home because it was the only day upon which he could play with the children. Another said he took no account of the churches but believed in being good, and "I ain't no atheist, either."[6] If the wife goes, the husband thinks he is well represented. Husband and wife rarely attend church together.

In several instances[7] the family said, as an excuse for non-church attendance, that their clothes were too shabby, or that they did not have the proper clothes. They prefer to stay at home rather than have their old acquaintances talk about their poverty.

The measure of church attendance is more or less the distance from the church. It is probably for this reason that the church membership is much lower west than east of Eleventh avenue.

---

[1] Monograph xviii. Besides the fear of a loss in social position, if the funeral is not "fine," may there not be also a dread of the implied lack of religious ceremony?
[2] Monograph xix. [3] Monograph xxiii [4] Monographs xvii, xxi. [5] Monograph xxiii.
[6] Monogaph xx. [7] Monographs xv, xix, xx.

The chief reasons for church attendance are: adherence to tradition and custom, a sense of duty, "it's everybody's duty to go to church and pray for the heathen,"[1] to set a good example for the children, "because the music is so nice," "it is good to have the church on your side,"[2] the "Sisters are good to us then at Christmas-time."[3]

Families went to a particular church because it was convenient; because the neighbors went there also;[4] because the ministers were nice, or gave clothes and candy to the children at Christmas. Little thought is given to the fact that they might be Methodists and still be attending an Episcopal or Baptist church. Sometimes they have no idea of what the particular sect they belonged to stands for.[5] One woman[6] who attended a Swedenborgian church, had never heard of Swedenborg. One young girl,[7] whose mother attended a Methodist church, would not go to it because "it was too quiet." Another girl, a Catholic,[8] went to a Protestant church on Sundays with "her gentleman friend" and attended the Catholic church alone during the week.

Sometimes the wedding party have a "spread" after they come home from church. It is followed by a day or two in Jersey, a visit to the "theátre" or music hall, a dance given by the bridegroom's "pals," a trip to Coney Island, etc. Then the married pair occupy their new rooms or board out until they have furnished their home.

Cases of intermarriage between Catholic and Protestant are not uncommon. The ceremony is usually performed in the Catholic Church. Sometimes the Protestant "turns Catholic." If he or she does not there is an agreement that each worship in his or her own way. Although there is an extraordinary disinclination to discuss questions of marriage and parenthood in general, there is, in such instances, an understanding about the religious education of future children.[9] It is made privately beforehand or it is mentioned in the marriage ceremony. The girls, as a rule, go to the mother's church, the boys "take after" the father. When there is a marriage between Catholic and Jew, the latter

---

[1] Monograph x. [2] Monograph xv. [3] Monographs ii, iii. [4] Monograph xiv.
[5] Monograph xiv. [6] Monograph x. [7] Monograph xvii. [8] Monographs vii, xvii.
[9] Monographs xiii, xvi, xviii.

usually gives up his faith.[1] One Jew was christened at his dying wife's bedside in order that he might join her in Heaven. His family have nothing more to do with him. The Protestant goes to "mass" or a Catholic church festival or jubilee.[2] The Catholic is less free about going to "another church."[3] A woman frequently takes a neighbor to the mother's guild of her church to "spend a pleasant evening." One woman[4] felt so sorry that there were so many sects. She said: "You're either a Christian or you aint." Others thought that "being[5] a Catholic or Protestant don't make no difference." "As long as you are good you get to Heaven just the same." One woman[6] said that a "Jew what kept his religion would get to Heaven."

The children are christened soon after birth. The Catholics christen before the end of the first week; the Lutherans, Episcopalians and Methodists within the first few months. A neighbor or a relative is asked to "stand for" the child. Except in a Catholic family, the godparent need not necessarily be a member of the church. When the child is named for a kinsman, the latter is supposed to make gifts to his godchild on birthdays, at Christmas and Easter.[7] When the family is in trouble[8] he is appealed to. The father seems to take little interest in the christening.[9] On the occasion several of the neighbors and friends accompany the mother to the church. One christening took place November, 1903, on a Sunday evening, at eight o'clock.[10] A "lady friend stood for" the six months' old infant. The godmother had given the infant a christening dress, coat, cap, etc., as was customary. The father did not go. The mother and three neighbors completed the party. During the middle of the regular service the sacrament was performed. The "godmother" walked down the aisle stood before the minister and held the child in her arms. The Lord's Prayer was repeated by the minister and then by the godmother. The child was anointed and was given the name of the "lady friend" by the express wish of the family. The day previous the mother had registered the child, godmother, etc. Another

---

[1] Monograph xxiv. [2] Monograph x. [3] Monograph vii. [4] Monograph x. [5] Monograph xiv. [6] Monograph iv. [7] Monographs x, xvi. [8] Monograph xvi. [9] Monographs xiv, xxi. [10] Monograph xiv.

hymn was sung, the mother was congratulated and the child was taken home.

The Sunday-school is chosen for about the same reason as the church. It is convenient. It keeps the children off the streets.[1] It gives the mother some rest. The house doesn't seem so full when they are gone. A neighbor's child went to a certain Sunday-school, so Florence went also.[2] It meant Christmas and Easter presents and a certain sense of protection. There was a chance that the child might be sent to the country during the next summer.[3] The children, as a rule, fail to go, only if they have been ill or have no clothes to wear.[4]

Both boy and girl take special afternoon instruction when they are old enough to be confirmed.[5] Confirmation is an expensive rite. It means new clothes, flowers, gifts, money to the church, etc. In this parish the confirmation of the Catholic child takes place only on alternate years when "the Bishop comes to town." First communion is also an impressive time in the young person's life. Fasting the whole day is required.[6]

Later on, the young man becomes a member of the boys' club connected with the church.[7] The girl may attend a sewing class. Sometimes both the boy and girl continue to attend graduate classes in the Sunday-school.

If possible Catholic parents send their children to one of the two parochial schools in the district. Several of them realize that the public school education is superior,[8] but they think "prayers and knowing the Bible comes first." Moreover, "the Sisters keep them off the street."[9]

Some of the residents pay pew rent. All contribute at least a small share for the poor and to foreign missions.

You attend the funeral of all your kinsfolk; "they expect it."[10] You have to get new mourning clothes, too, and they "cost."[11] You send flowers, and go in your own carriage, if possible. A coach to Calvary cemetery "costs me nine dollars,"[12] one woman said. "You get out and stand on the damp ground during the burial services, 'cause folks would talk if you stayed in the

---

[1] Monograph x. [2] Monograph xv. [3] Monograph xxi. [4] Monographs viii, xx.
[5] Monographs viii, xvi. [6] Monograph xvi. [7] Monographs v, x. [8] Monographs viii, xvi, xx. [9] Monograph ii. [10] Monographs iii, iv, x, xv. [11] Monograph xv.
[12] Monograph iv.

carriage."[1] The funeral display is an indication of a person's social status. His funeral must be as "fine" as his neighbors'. All things are sacrificed in order to avoid pauper burial. If the neighbors hear that there is going to be a pauper burial, one of them goes around for a subscription and the required sum is soon raised. A mother[2] wishes to "bury her dead boy as good as any rich man's son."

For the Catholic wake the Lutheran has a hearty contempt.[3] "There is smoking and drinking and nice carryin's on in the kitchen." The Protestant wake is entirely different. It is "simply watching by the coffin, not a party." No matter what your faith is you go to your neighbor's wake.

One woman, an Episcopalian,[4] whose husband was an orthodox Jew, considered it "low and vulgar" to discuss doctrinal questions. The men seldom discuss religious questions, although they swear with anthropomorphic familiarity. All hold to the traditional views of Heaven, Hell and Purgatory. The Catholics, especially, dwell upon the future state in their talk. There is an implicit belief that all that is done is done well. It is a sin even to think of controlling the sex of the unborn child. "That's a matter which ought to be left entirely in God's hands."[5] The dead child is with the angels or is one himself. The sinner still has a chance to redeem himself on his deathbed. "God may take me if He wishes to,"[6] or "God's will be done." Modern science is not welcome. "We hear[7] that there is some that preach that man comes from a monkey. We know that God made man; it's written in His word."

ATTITUDE TOWARDS PHYSICIANS, HOSPITALS, ETC.

The Irish frequently speak of the physician as a "charmer." On one occasion a man with a severe cold went to the "charmer" to be cured. The latter "pulled out his hair as mauch as a cap could cover; roasted two eggs and put them on the bald spot, then he muttered to himself, when he got through the man could swaller and holler as loud as any one." "In the owld country"

---

1 Monograph vii. 2 Monograph vii. 3 Monograph xiii. 4 Monograph xxiv.
5 Monograph viii. 6 Monograph vii. 7 Monograph iv.

when a person has a sore throat ("they call it dipthery here") "the charmer takes a frog, ties a string to him and lets him go up and down till he takes out the lump." In some cases the physicians of New York city are regarded as quacks "who don't come up to the Irish charmer."[1]

The Irish Catholic mother believes that praying over a sick child will cure it and placing "holy bones" on the body of a crippled child will make it whole. In Ireland there is a church where even the blind are "cured."[2] One woman has seen cripples walk out of the church "just like other people."[3] The men of the family do not, as a rule, care to call in the doctor unless it is absolutely necessary. They prefer "to let things go on." Often a man will go without telling his family that he is sick. "The women folks do not understand men anyway."[4] As a usual thing the man also avoids hospitals and clinics. Sometimes he goes and doesn't tell his wife about it.[5]

Usually a "pay" doctor is preferred as a matter of pride, and because he "gives more attention to the patient." One woman[6] had an alopath for herself and a homœpath for the children, "because he used home cures." For general illnesses "she saved" and used patent medicines. The usual charges of a "pay" doctor are from a dollar to a dollar fifty. One woman[7] refused to go to a "pay doctor" in " 'Arlem" because "he charged two dollars a visit and that's special rates and without medicine at that." The charges for services at confinement are regularly ten dollars.

I have known of cases in which the woman refused to go to a man physician to explain their "female troubles." One woman[8] felt sick before the birth of her child, but she was "ashamed" to consult a man doctor so she went to a "lady doctor." Most of the women say that they have been "opirated" for "female troubles." Sometimes[9] a girl is taken to a "lady doctor who

---

[1] This is especially true in the case of those suffering from tuberculosis. It will be interesting to see how the free circulation of the pamphlets prepared by the Committee on Tuberculosis by the Charity Organization Society will affect this attitude. The women whom I knew were glad to get the pamphlets; they showed them to their neighbors also.
[2] Monograph xix. [3] Monograph iii. [4] Monograph v. [5] Monograph xiv. [6] Monograph xxi. [7] Monograph i. [8] Monograph xxiii. [9] Monographs vii, xvii.

advertises" a "sure cure" within a specified time "or your money back."

Numerous patent medicines are in use to cure illnesses, as "Rickey's Drug Bargains" or "Doctor Humphrey's Patent Medicines." The father of the family will secretly go off to a doctor who cures consumption in a week "or your money back."[1]

Occasionally there is a "family doctor."[2] His choice is purely fortuitous. In one case of confinement a doctor was called in because he lived around the corner.[3] The doctor had come from a dinner. He was intoxicated and did not give the right kind of help. As a result, the patient states that she has suffered from "piles" ever since. (Of course she has used every "pile cure" in existence.) Nevertheless she continued to employ the same doctor for a number of years.

In another case[4] the doctor's instruments, according to the mother, distorted the shape of the child's head. "The baby died from this," but the mother continued to call in the same doctor. In this same family, in the case of a later confinement, the "Fifth Avenue doctor" had been engaged beforehand. The physician took no interest because "we was poor;" he was careless and the "head bones" were driven together. "The eyes had an extra skin over them." "It was the doctor's fault that Annie's sight is queer."

In one case a woman was with difficulty persuaded to change her physician. She preferred the inefficient one because he "told her things."[5]

The physician is not engaged many weeks before confinement. One mother never engages the midwife until the day before.[6] The mother usually says "what's the sense, he'll come round soon enough."

Little provision is made for the coming of the child. In one case[7] in which an expectant mother was persuaded to make clothes for the baby a few months in advance, the neighbors said "the bank ladies are sometimes queer." Midwives are employed more frequently than physicians. They receive from one dollar to two

---

1 Monograph xiv. 2 Monographs iv, v. 3 Monograph iv. 4 Monograph viii.
5 Monograph xiv. 6 Monograph ii. 7 Monograph xiv.

dollars a day for their services. They "wash the baby and clean up besides." Again the family engages a doctor for a day or two and one of the neighbors acting as a nurse tends to things after that.[1] Frequently a neighbor will play the part of midwife regardless of the law, at a lower rate than charged by the licensed midwife. The residents also refer to the practice of unlicensed doctors in the neighborhood. The mother is " 'round again"[2] within a surprisingly short time. Even when the woman would like to apply to a Maternity Hospital, the husband objects on the ground that "those are for them that don't know better." One woman reluctantly said[3] that she went to the "Woman's Hospital" once when she was too poor to pay anything. Another woman[4] applied at the Sloan Maternity Hospital.

One woman told me that her husband went out at the eleventh hour to "fetch the doctor."[5] The baby was born before he came. No one was at hand "so she washed the baby herself just as good as the doctor would have."

One woman[6] attends to her newly-born infants herself, because "men don't know about them things as well as women do."

The word hospital is often tabooed. If you say clinic or dispensary the patient will go more willingly. All the women give as one reason for their not going to hospitals is the fact that the young doctors and students use them to experiment on, as "if poor folks didn't have any feeling."

There is a tendency to change hospitals very frequently. Sometimes the family doesn't know the name of the hospital where one of its members is being cared for. One woman[7] did not know whether she had taken "Eddie" to the Babies' Hospital or Saint Mary's.

In another case in which I had sent the child to the Opthalmic Hospital, the mother forgot where the hospital was, lost the card and could not go to see "Mary" until I had given her the address.[8] Again[9] I gave a mother two addresses and marked one as especially desirable. Another time the same mother could not decide between the Nursery and Childs' Hospital and Vanderbilt

---

1 Monograph vii. 2 Monographs x, xviii. 3 Monograph xix. 4 Monograph xiii.
5 Monograph xviii. 6 Monograph xviii. 7 Monograph xvii. 8 Monograph xiv.
9 Monograph xvi.

Clinic. There is a tendency to change hospitals very frequently without good reason. "If he goes to both he may get cured quicker," she said. I took one child to the Manhattan Eye and Ear Hospital several times myself. Then the mother took him. She "did not like the looks of the place" so she took him to the New Amsterdam Eye and Ear Hospital. After a few weeks of treatment there she grew tired of the doctor, so she took the child to Saint Bartholomew's Hospital.

The interference of the Board of Health in the case of contagious diseases is still resented to a certain degree, although the attitude towards this department has undergone a considerable change during the past years. More residents call in "the health doctor." Moreover, the families are so accustomed now to being inspected or visited that they do not seem to resent it any more. "It spoils the furniture, pastes up the windows and keeps the children separated just when the sick child wants company most."[1] Besides "it is foolish to have the other children miss school." One boy[2] was sent to work in a laundry when the other children had the measles. When there is a case of serious illness the neighbors call to show their sympathy. The neighbors' children invariably come in also. "There aint no room in our house and 'Annie' next door aint so sick but what she wants to play with the children."[3] Very soon the disease spreads through the whole house and sometimes even to the next house. One woman[4] did not wish a case of scarlet fever reported. She preferred to keep her child at home. She thought the others would not be "likely to get it." The mother also leaves the milk uncovered and meat exposed when there is a case of contagious disease.[5] Frequently cases are not reported when the mother thinks that the child will be removed from the house. Some mothers think that the action of the Board of Health in vaccinating children of a school age is an infringement on the rights of the parent. One woman[6] showed the health doctor the door, and he didn't dare to come back."

---

[1] Monograph xvi. [2] Monograph xvi. [3] Monograph ii. [4] Monograph xxiii.
[5] Monographs v, xxiii. [6] Monograph xviii.

ATTITUDE TOWARDS POLICE DEPARTMENT.

The attitude towards the Police Department varies. "They are a bad lot."[1] "They only like the man who keeps his hand out behind his back." "They are simply on the force for what they can get out of it."[2] Or, "they are your friends." The "corner cop" is an important personage and commands respect. He can enter a saloon or he can "shut an eye to the goings on." He can maintain order and prevent street fights. Everybody seems to know him and he knows everybody. The young men would like to emulate him because he has an easy job, gets a good salary and is insured a pension. The women know that he is their interpreter if the children are arrested for breaking windows or making bonfires. He is the children's friend. The boys wish they had a "big club," too. The girls[3] like the "grand blue suit and brass buttons." The women make use of him, too. One woman[4] threatens to call in the "cop" when her husband beats her.

The women have a horror of being summoned to court or having any connection with the police station. They do not go to court for divorce because it costs too much. Occasionally[5] they report cases of their own initiative to the Gerry Society, but such occurrences are rare; they prefer to "let things drag on."

POLITICAL IDEAS AND PRACTICES.

The women know little about their husbands' politics. The men refuse to talk about such subjects to them. "They are not meant for women folks."[6] One man, when asked by his wife how he voted, said: I would not even tell my father that."[7] As a rule, however, the women care not at all how their husbands' vote.

In several cases I found that the emigrant had not become a citizen. One man hoped to go back to Germany.[8] Another did not bother[9] about the first papers.

The men do not attend primaries, as a rule, because they are managed so skilfully in the district that "it makes no difference

---

1 Monograph xx.   2 Monograph xv.   3 Monograph x.   4 Monograph xv.
5 Monograph xvii.   6 Monograph v.   7 Monograph iii.   8 Monograph xvi.
9 Monograph xiv.

whether you go or not."[1] The primaries are too complicated for the poor man. They are meant for the clever politician.

The residents speak about the great amount of election bribery that goes on. One man told me that he had had the strength to refuse a bribe of five dollars.[2] He spoke of it as though it were a rather unusual act. "The boys had their laugh on me, but I'm an honest man." That man was out of work and his rent was due two months.

The choice of the party is a sentimental one. The district "boss" is more successful in getting out men to vote than any educational influence or institution could possibly be, for he knows how to minister to the social and individual needs of his ward. He pays the rent of the dispossessed man. He finds work[3] for him. He gives bail when the poor man is fined. He invites whole families to annual picnics.[4] He buys tickets for the benefit entertainment. He attends the funerals. He pays funeral expenses. He invites the neighbors "to a drink," or a supper, and he gets a "pass" for a man going on a journey. Upon these and other "kindnesses not worth talking about" depends a man's vote.

RELATIONS TO NEIGHBORS.

The readiness to give and share seems to me to be one of the chief traits in the relation of neighbor to neighbor. The aid given is of a simple kind. It satisfies an immediate need. Above all it is spontaneous. Your neighbor, no matter how cold the night runs across the street to help nurse your neighbor's dying child.[5] Or she washes the body of the dead child in preparation for burial.[6] If she lives on the floor above she sends her own children to a relative for quiet.[7] She helps watch all night.[8] She comes to the wake, attends the funeral and if she knows the family at all well she goes out to the cemetery with the bereaved. Again she tends you during confinement without pay, and even goes so far as to take home the other children "to have 'em out of the way."[9] In recognition of her goodness she is asked to be godmother.

---

[1] Monograph xv. [2] Monograph xv. [3] Monograph xiii. [4] Monographs v, x, xvii.
[5] Monographs ii, x. [6] Monograph xiv. [7] Monograph xx. [8] Monograph ii.
[9] Monographs x, xvii.

When a mother has to go out for the day she "leaves" the children with her neighbor or asks her to go in "and have a look at them."[1] The neighbor comes in when the children are sick, she offers her blankets, makes some soup, suggests her own physician or brings cakes and goodies to the sick child. She visits a neighbor patient in the hospital and brings her ice cream and candy or flowers.[2] If a mother dies suddenly, a neighbor takes the children to her own rooms. If a child is neglected she takes her "for months and asks no board."[3] The young girl on the same floor is given a place in the home "to keep her from fallin' into[4] low company." If your husband gets "drunk" a neighbor opens[5] her door to you. If you get separated or dispossessed "she has always room for one more."[6]

The neighbors lend every thing they have from the kettle or coffee pot to their best black skirt for a funeral. One woman lent her christening robe nineteen times.[7] Your neighbor is even willing to lend money "unless you are false to her,"[8] but in that case there would "be an end of it even if you went down on your knees." You are thought "stingy"[9] if you wont give as much as you can.

As a rule all the families in a house know one another either intimately or at least by sight. They know each other's needs to the most intimate details. There is little privacy in the house. Your neighbor meets you in the hall or she "hollers up the shaft to you." I have known of cases in which women are always visiting "and don't know when to stay away." The neighbor's children "run in and out" all day long.

Some of the families, on the other hand, see little of their neighbors either in the house or on the street.[10] One woman complained that they were coarse and rough.[11] She would not allow her children to associate with them. One man calls the neighbors "a tough lot" and says that "the street has changed."[12] His family go with only a few who come in "for a drink." The people[13] in the house have "dropped them," "for they keep low company and respectable folks ought to have nothing to do with them. They just starve their children." One woman said she used to

---

1 Monographs xiv, xvi.   2 Monograph v.   3 Monographs xiii, xvii.   4 Monograph i.
5 Monograph xii.   6 Monograph xx.   7 Monograph ii.   8 Monograph xviii.   9 Monograph vii.
10 Monographs iii, vi, viii.   11 Monograph xxiv.   12 Monograph xx.   13 Monograph iv.

know "everybody in Forty-sixth street."[1] She does not "follow them up any longer." Besides she does not find time "to gossip like some do," and she stays at home "nights" with her husband and does not visit "except her relations." One man said "the crowd in the house are brawlers" and make such a noise that he can not sleep at night.[2] Another resident considered herself "too good to go with the people in the house."[3] "They were people of no education." "They quarreled and drank and got into street fights and their children ran around loose." Another resident was unsociable because she "was ashamed of letting people know the goings on in her house."[4] She always kept the door locked and complained that the neighbors did not know "how to mind their own business." One German mother said that she had no time to "go visiting all day long and the children kept her busy."[5] One young American-born girl[6] would not look at any of the women in the house. "They let their pans go uncleaned and their skirts drag in the street. No wonder their children are like them."

II

TABLE OF WAGE-EARNING AND OCCUPATIONS OF MEMBERS OF MONOGRAPH FAMILIES.

No. of Monograph.	Position in Family.	Occupation.	Wages and Time of Employment.
I	Son, aged 31 Son, aged 29	Japanner Trunk factory	$7.00 a week. $5.00 a week.
II	F. Daughter, aged 21	Marble polisher Housemaid	$3.00 a day; 3–4 days during week. $12.00 a month.
III	Son, aged 38	Fishman	$6.00–$8.00 a week.
IV	Son, aged 54 Daughter, aged 41	Printer Laundress	$12.00–$15.00 a week. $0.75–$1.00 a day; 5 days of week.
V	Son, aged 25 Daughter, aged 30 Daughter, aged 17	Letter carrier Laundress Trunk factory	$50.00 a month. $1.00 a day; 2 days of week. $3.50 a week.

[1] Monograph ii. [2] Monograph xv. [3] Monograph xvi. [4] Monograph iv. [5] Monograph x. [6] Monograph vii.

TABLE OF WAGE-EARNING, ETC.—Continued.

No. of Monograph.	Position in Family.	Occupation.	Wages and Time of Employment.
VI	Daughter Son-in-law	Laundress Carpet factory hand	$1.00 a day. $7.20 a week.
VII	M. Daughter, aged 21	Office cleaner Laundry work	$5.00 a week. $5.00 a week.
VIII	F. Son, aged 15 Daughter, aged 16	Derrick lifter Carpet factory hand Carpet factory hand	$2.00–$3.00 a day; idle in winter months. $8.00 a week. $5.00 a week.
IX	F.	Laborer	$1.75 a day.
X	F. M. Son, aged 19 Son, aged 17	Bookbinder Takes care of charge baby Occasional washing Farm hand since May, 1905 Errand and office boy	$12.00 a week. $8.00 a month (not paid after April, 1905.) $1.00 a day; 2 days of week. Not paid, although promised $12.00 a month. $5.50 a week.
XI	Grandmother M. F.	Chambermaid Laundress For support of daughter	$18.00 a month, irregularly. $0.75 a day, irregularly. $2.00 a week.
XII	M.	Laundress	$1.00 a day.
XIII	F.	Porter	$10.50 a week.
XIV	M. Daughter, aged 14	Laundress Paster	$1.00 a day; 5 days of week. $2.50 a week.
XV	F. M. Daughter, aged 15 Daughter, aged 14	Carpet factory worker Charwoman Minds baby Minds baby	$4.00 a week, irregularly. $1.00–$2.00 weekly. $0.50–$1.00 weekly. $0.50–$1.00 weekly.
XVI	M. Son, aged 14 Son, aged 10	"Helper" in day nursery Office boy Errand boy	$2.00 a week. $3.50 a week. $2.50 a week.
XVII	M. Daughter, aged 20	Takes care of three charge babies Silk factory hand	$10.00 a month for each. $5.00 a week, works irregularly.

TABLE OF WAGE-EARNING, ETC.—Continued.

No of Monograph	Position in Family.	Occupation.	Wages and Time of Employment.
XVIII	F.	Job carpenter	$4.00 a day; works 3 days of week.
	M.	Laundress	$0.75–$1.00 a day.
XIX	F.	Motor man	$18.00 a week; usually intoxicated 2 days a week; brings wife $12.00–$15.00 a week.
	Daughter, aged 19	Bakery	$3.50–$5.00, irregularly.
XX	F.	Bridge builder; out of work 1903–04	$2.50–$3.50 a day.
	M.	Scrubbing woman	$0.75–$1.25 a day.
XXI	F.	Driver	$15.00 a week in winter, $7.00 a week in summer.
XXII	F.	Laborer	$1.40 a day.
	M.	Laundress	$0.50–$1.00 a day.
XXIII	F.	Piano factory worker	$15.00 a week.
XXIV	F.	Potato peddler	$9.00 a week.

NOTE ON MEMBERSHIP IN TRADE UNIONS AND BENEFIT SOCIETIES.

I found few instances of membership in trade unions. The men with whom I discussed the subject said that they "do not believe in them," that "they did more harm than good," that "the initiation fee was too big," that "they result in strikes which cause misery and shut out men who want to work." Benefit associations seem to have greater attraction. I found members in the Odd Fellows' Lodge, Foresters' Lodge, Lodge of the Maccabees, Brotherhood of Carpenters, Order of the Ancient Hibernians, Red Rangers, Village Rangers, Lodge of the Red Men, etc.

INDUSTRIES.

The following table compiled from the 18th Annual Report of Factory Inspection, published in the Report of the New York Department of Labor for 1903, enumerates the larger industries of the district:

Butchers' fixtures	1	Ribbon factories	2
Bonnet wire	2	Soaps and perfumes	2
Bottling beer and soda	3	Stage properties	3
Button factory	1	Skylights	1
Cleaning and dyeing	2	Twine and ropes	2
Carpet factories	5	Trunks and bags	1
Carpenter shops	6	Trusses	1
Cigar factory	2	Tin work	1
Coach lamp	1	Varnish and paint	1
Disinfectants	1	Wire for screens	1
Decorative leather	1	Wood carving	1
Electric supplies	1	Willow Baskets	1
Glue and paste	1	Wire railings	1
Gas meters	1	Wagons and carriages	3
Harness	3	Umbrella covering	1
Ice	1	Upholstering	6
Iron work	4	Clothing and repairing establishments (Jews)	32
Mattresses	4	Laundry	18
Picture frames	1	Dressmakers	14
Printing stores	4	Bakeries	10
Piano factories	5		
Piano harness and appliances	3		

The employés of these industries and of the much larger number of smaller unenumerated industries live, as a rule, in the district.

OUT OF WORK.

There were several cases of lack of employment because of a builders' strike. In some departments of the building trade there is always "slack times" or no work in the winter months. The men know about this beforehand, but they refuse to work at something else for lower wages. Sometimes they do not even look for another job.[1] In several cases the husband was offered work in the woodyard[2] and at street-cleaning.[3] He refused to take the job; it was "beneath him." The men either sit at home and, as one German woman said, "refuse to put on their shoes,"[4] or they go to the saloon and spend a day in loafing. The American-born boy who is out of work frequently avoids the saloon on such occasions.[5] If they leave the house at five-thirty or six in the morning and find no work they come home discouraged; then it is the wife who has the hardest time. When the lack

---

[1] Monograph viii.   [2] Monograph v.   [3] Monograph xx.   [4] Monograph x.
[5] Monographs iv, v. vii.

of employment continues she may "take a hand" herself, and scrub, clean or "wash out" to keep[1] the children from starving. The grocer gives credit for a surprisingly long time and for a large sum, twenty to thirty dollars. The "boss" advanced the wages of the next summer in one case.[2] The landlord waits for the rent.[3] The neighbors send up the left-overs or give the children a part of their own dinner.[4] Often they bring in the clothes their own children have outgrown. The rich lady[5] "what mamma works for" also sends down things or the Sister gives the children shoes and material for a dress. (These are pawned almost immediately.) Sometimes the case is put in the hands of the Charity Organization Society or the Society for Improving the Condition of the Poor.[6]

The furniture is not valuable enough to mortgage, but articles of clothing, and in some cases special pieces of furniture, have been taken to "hock."[7] The articles are taken to "uncle's" early in the morning. The neighbors must not know about it. The church visitor must not be told. The penny provident visitor finds out by merest chance from the children. The children are not sent begging, but they are forced to work. If the family accepts charitable aid, they will be socially ostracized. So they prefer to starve along in dependence on their children, rather than get free groceries, and continue to send the children to school.

FAMILY EXPENDITURE.

About one-half of the family income goes for food. There might be a considerable saving of expenditure if women knew more about food values, and the possibilities of making use of "left overs" from a previous meal. The poorer the family, the more wasteful the mother seems to be. She buys too much in many instances and wastes over half. She does not keep a market book or remember what she has bought. Usually she pays for each purchase immediately. She buys in small quantities when it would be cheaper to buy in large amounts. She would have, to be sure, no place to store supplies.

One-quarter of the income goes for rent, the average rent being from eight dollars to ten dollars. In 1903-4 the rent was

---

[1] Monographs xii, xx.   [2] Monograph viii.   [3] **Monographs viii, xii, xiv.**
[4] **Monograph iv.**   [5] Monograph xx.   [6] Monographs xi, xix.   [7] **Monographs xv, xvi.**

going up steadily in the neighborhood. A family had to pay fifty cents to a dollar more for the same rooms. It prevented the usual moving fever in some instances. When the family was "hard up," concessions were made, but the new tenant was "raised."

Less than a quarter is thus left for clothing and recreation. The mother is willing to make great sacrifices to give her oldest daughter a new dress for the next "racket." Not uncommonly she must be well dressed for she is "keeping company." There must be money for life insurance. The family must contribute to the church. The father wants "beer money." He also wants something to enable him to fill his pipe. If there is illness, money is needed for doctor and medicines. Too frequently the family diet is cut down in order that the things that "show" may be bought.

A Characteristic Table of Expenditure During One Month, February 17 to March 18, 1904.[1]

Feb. 17 Rolls, .10; milk, .05; flour, .04; eggs, .10; jelly, .10; cakes, .10; herring, .15—$0.64.

Feb. 18 Rolls, .10; chop and suet, .21; potatoes, .10; peas, .05; cakes, .05; milk, .05; sandwiches, .05; eggs, .07; bread, .08—$0.76.

Feb. 19 Rolls, .10; milk, .05; butter, .08; cheese, .15; bread, .09—$0.47.

Feb. 20 Rolls, .10; milk, .05; soup meat, 0.15; suet, .05; soup greens. .05; barley, .02; lemons, .05; veal, .25; macaroni, .10; coffee, .20; cheese, .10; bread, .10; sandwich and pickle, .05—$1.27.

Feb. 21 Coffee cake, 15; milk, .05; butter, .07; apples and oranges, .10—$0.37.

Feb. 22 Rolls, .10; stewing beef, .15; potatoes, .10; cakes, .10; macaroni, .10; tomatoes, .10; milk, .05—$0.70.

Feb. 23 Rolls, .10; milk, .05; soup greens and suet, .20; apples, .02; rice, 02; bread, .09; onions, .02; delicatessen, .12—$0.62.

Feb. 24 Rolls, .10; milk, .05; flour, .12; bananas, .02; cheese, .10; bread, .10—$0.49.

Feb. 25 Rolls, .10; corned beef, .28; milk, .05; potatoes, .10; beans, .10; cake, 10; cheese, 10; bread, .09; jelly, .10—$1.02.

Feb. 26 Rolls, .10; milk, .05; butter, .08; delicatessen, .20; bread, .09; sugar, .06—$0.58.

Feb. 27 Rolls, .10; milk, .05; delicatessen, .15; cake, .10; cold supper, .15; meat, .25; coffee, .20; sugar, .16—$1.16.

---

[1] Monograph xvi.

Feb. 28 Macaroni, .10; cereal, .15; milk, .05; soup meat, .10; crackers, .10—$0.50.
Feb. 29 Rolls, .10; milk, .05; meat, .16; potatoes, .10; butter, .05; onions, .05; bread, .10; delicatessen, .15; beer, .05—$0.81.
Mar. 1 Rolls, .10; milk, .05; liver, .10; macaroni, .10; tomatoes, .06; apples, .06—$0.47.
Mar. 2 Rolls, .10; milk, .05; eggs, .16; milk, .05; ice cream, .10; oranges, .06; butter, .17; bread, .08—$0.77.
Mar. 3 Rolls, .05; milk, .05; stewing beef, .15; eggs, .06; potatoes, .10; bread, .05; oranges, .04—$0.50.
Mar. 4 Rolls, .10; milk, .05; chowder, .10; crackers, .05; bread, .10; onions, .15; oranges, .05; ham, .10—$0.70.
Mar. 5 Rolls, .10; milk, .05; soup meat, .15; soup greens, .05; rice, .04; oranges, .04; cake, .05; milk, .05; sausage, .05—$0.58.
Mar. 6 Coffee cake, .15; milk, .05; macaroni, .10; delicatessen, .10; —$0.40.
Mar. 7 Rolls, .10; milk, .05; bread, .08, lentils, .08; butter, .08; coffee, .20; bone of ham, .10—$0.69.
Mar. 8 Rolls, .10; milk, .05; steak and suet, .22; potatoes, .10; corn, .12; delicatessen, .15—$0.74.
Mar. 9 Rolls, .10; milk, .05; chowder, .15; crackers, .05; eggs, .10; cake, .05; milk, .05—$0.55.
Mar. 10 Rolls, .10; milk, .05; beef for stew, .15; suet, .05; potatoes, .10; delicatessen, .10; bread, .09; butter, .07—$0.71.
Mar. 12 Rolls, .05; soup meat, .15; greens, .05; milk, .05; cake, .05; macaroni, .10; cheese, .05; herring, .04; bread, .05; potatoes, .10; turnip, .10; meat, .25—$1.04.
Mar. 13 Coffee cake, .15; delicatessen, .10—$0.25.
Mar. 14 Rolls, .10; milk, .05; pork chops, .15; potatoes, .10; cake, .05; cheese, .10; butter, .07; onions, .02—$0.64.
Mar. 15 Rolls, .05; milk, .08; liver, .10; bacon, .05; cake, .05; bread, .05; sausage, .10; flour, .12—$0.60.
Mar. 16 Rolls, .10; milk, .05; eggs, .15; sugar and butter, .12; cakes, .05; eggs, .10; bread, .05—$0.62.
Mar. 17 Rolls, .10; milk, .05; stewing beef, .15; potatoes, .10; cakes, .05; milk, .05—$0.50.
Mar. 18 Rolls, .10; milk, .05; eggs, .10; bread, .05; milk, .05; butter, .07—$0.42.

Total...$19.57

Clothing			
Gloves	$0.10	White waist	.98
Underwear	.25	Black waist	.98
Stockings	.77	Umbrella	.98
Garters	.26	Easter hat	1.88
Shoes	1.69	Belt	.25
Corset	.49	Total	$8.63

Other Necessaries			
Scissors	$0.20	Church money	.30
Thimble	.05	Sunday papers	.45
Thread	.20	Writing paper	.50
Pocketbook	.10	Carfare	1.22
School-bag	.25	Lent neighbors	.40
Slate and pencils	.07		
Drawing map	.05	Total	$6.83
Atomizer	.59	Food	$18.83
Medicines	.25	Clothing	8.98
Shoe polish	.20	Rent	8.50
Shoe laces	.02	Gas	1.50
Washing powder	.13	Coal and Wood	3.52
Oil	.11	Life insurance, .30 weekly	1.12
Soap	.10	Other necessaries	7.83
Camphorated oil	.14		
Music	1.50	Total	$50.28

Income

Allowance from father-in-law in Germany	$29.63
Fee for playing a violin obligato at a church concert	10.00
Earnings of eldest child, age	3.40
"Hocking" the violin	6.00
Total	$49.03

SAVINGS.

As a rule there were few instances of savings except for special purposes, the purchase of a gas stove, a sewing machine, a piano, etc. I was able to persuade several women[1] to open a regular bank account however. Usually they prefer their stocking or the mattress as a safe deposit vault. The wages were too small in most cases to expect saving; the family lives from hand to mouth. They consume almost immediately what they earn.

I have come to wonder not why more families are able to save, but how it is that they manage to get along as well as they do. Incidentally I might say that, nevertheless, the system of penny provident collecting is a fruitful one. The result of urging the children to save, by getting them interested in having as many pretty colored stamps as possible is in almost all cases successful. Saving means a lesson in self-restraint, for no candy, ice-cream,

---
[1] Monographs x, xiv, xvii.

cake or pickle can be bought during the week. It means "saving up" for a warm winter coat, for medicines in time of illness or for a Christmas present for father and mother. A friendly rivalry arises between members of the same family. Frequently the mother also begins to save. In one instance[1] where the father was always out when I called, he finally forbade my visits. Several weeks later his stepdaughter wrote for me to come. Before long the man himself saved. I gave him the stamps on the stairs for he wished to surprise his wife at Christmas.

In one case a young woman asked me whether I would allow her "gentleman friend" to deposit through her.[2]

INSURANCE.

Life or rather burial insurance is an item of expense invariably found among the Irish and German families of the district. The fear of a plain pine box and cheap shroud and rest on Hart's Island makes life insurance a necessity. I found only one case[3] in which a man "didn't see much in it." Everyone in the family over a year old is insured. Sometimes the children are actually starved in order to pay the premium. In case of the death of the head of the family, all the insurance is used for a "fine funeral" and in order to buy mourning clothes for the survivors. The father and mother are insured for fifteen cents a week. The other adult members pay ten cents; the children five.

Usually the wife chooses the company and pays for her husband and children. Sometimes an adult son pays his own premium to a different company. Sometimes the husband is insured in two different companies.[4] One woman didn't know in which company her husband was insured.[5] Another one paid her husband's insurance although she had been separated from him for years.[6]

One woman[7] was anxious to give her husband a "big funeral" in spite of the fact that she did not think he deserved it. She was persuaded with difficulty to give me the insurance money for safekeeping. She received two hundred and twenty-nine dollars.

---

1 Monograph xvii.   2 Monograph ii.   3 Monograph iii.   4 Monograph xvii.
5 Monograph xix.   6 Monograph vii.   7 Monograph xiv.

It is not so much the evil of insurance itself as the lack of knowledge of how much to spend (including infant life insurance) and the greater evil of the extortionate charges of the undertaker. There is a great need for an association which would supervise and regulate insurance and funeral charges among the poor.

Of this she took a hundred dollars for funeral expenses, as the neighbors would talk if she didn't give him a "fine layout." The house was cleaned, the curtains were washed and the choicest ornaments were set out. The family bought mourning clothes, an "entire set" for each member. The body was placed in the living room. The friends and neighbors sat in the kitchen, which had been converted into a sitting-room. No food was cooked until after the funeral. The wife employed a "funeral director" in the neighborhood, a man who was patronized by all her friends. He was not connected with any church. His bill read as follows:

Grave (in Lutheran cemetery)	$20.00
Coffin	27.00
Embalming	10.00
Shroud (he called this giving the shroud away)	2.00
Black hearse	10.00
Two carriages	13.00
Shaving	2.00
Attendance	1.50
Top board	1.50
Transcript of death	.75
Total	$88.25

The black *crepe* with the white ribbons and wax flowers at the door were "free." The horses were decorated with white ribbons "so as to make a fine show." The lunch at the cemetery amounted to three dollars and twenty-five cents.

A TYPICAL APARTMENT.

The apartment consists of three rooms in a twenty-five foot, four-story house, with similar tenement houses on both sides and in the rear. There are three other like apartments on the same floor.

The dimensions and lighting of the rooms follow:

(1) Kitchen, 7 x 10, lighted by air-shaft and window opening out into hall.

(2) Living and bedroom, 10 x 15, lighted by two front windows.

(3) Bedroom (front room), 6 x 7, lighted by one front window.

(A small, dark closet is off the kitchen. It is used for storing old furniture, rags, wood, etc.)

There is no bath in the house. There are four water-closets in the yard. Each closet is used by three families, who are expected to take turns in keeping it clean. Each family has a key.

The water supply consists of one faucet with sink in the hallway, plus one-fauceted sink in the kitchen. There is a stationary tub in the kitchen. The drying of the clothes is done on a "family rope" in the back yard. In the hallway there is a single globeless gas jet. The jets are not kept lighted during the day, consequently the halls are very dark. The family store their coal and wood in the cellar if they buy in large quantities. Usually, they buy "by the pail."

In the kitchen stands a small cooking stove, near which is a coal scuttle and ash pan, a movable wooden washtub and a stationary washtub and sink; above this is a wooden shelf for kitchen utensils and dishes. They consist of less than a dozen plates, cups and saucers, a large bowl, two platters, several glasses, a tea and coffee pot and several frying pans. On the kitchen table stand an oil lamp and a medley of pots, pans, dishes, combs, brushes, shoe polish, etc. Under the table, a basket of potatoes and the "store" of green groceries find a place. In a corner the broom and scrubbing brush are placed. On the door leading into the storage closet is a roller for towels. On another shelf are the clock and some china figures. Above this hangs the motto "God Bless Our Home."

In the living and bedroom stands a large wooden wardrobe, which contains all the family clothes, treasures, cast-off clothing, etc. Next to this is the bureau (so near that one can hardly open the bureau drawers). On the bureau is the family shrine, a brown wooden box with a slanting roof. In this there is an image of the Virgin, over whom is hung a rosary. The family Bible and a picture of Saint Anthony are also placed on the bureau. On the mantelpiece there are a brown wooden clock, several brightly colored vases filled with artificial flowers, two glass crucifixes, a china image of the Virgin, a plaster image of Mary with the infant Jesus and some gaudy calendars. In front of the mantel is a table covered with a red tablecloth on which are placed soiled and clean clothes, shoes, school-books, iron, soap, hammer and nails, a scrubbing brush, dolls, etc. Next to the mantle is a large white enamel folding-bed. Between the windows on the north wall there is a mirror. Against the west wall are placed the ironing board, a sewing machine, some broken chairs and a rocker. On the walls hang colored pictures of Saint Benedict and Christ Healing the Sick, a newspaper print of Pope Leo XIII and of Pope Pius; a photograph of a family tombstone in Ireland; a colored print of a praying child and several insurance, grocer and brewery calendars. Over the mantel hangs a chromo of the father in a bright gilt frame decorated by palm leaves. On either side hang bright prints of saints, also a picture of a young woman and child under a shower of apple blossoms. On the north wall is the rest of the family portrait gallery, a chromo of the wife's sister, a tintype framed in gold of the wife's mother, a photograph of the wife's dead brother, and pictures of the husband's parents and sister.

A door opens on the west side of this room to the smaller bedroom. There the furniture consists of a large double bed, a stand with a washbowl, a small table on which stands a wooden crucifix and a mirrorless bureau. The walls are decorated with bright pictures of angels and saints.

A family of eight, the parents and six children, live in this apartment.[1]

HOUSEKEEPING.

Some of the homes which I visited were spotlessly clean. The bed linen was changed, the clothes were washed and the rooms cleaned with regularity. In others, chiefly the homes of the underfed and overburdened, the mother, the household drudge, had lost interest, or there were so many children that she never had "a chance to clean." In these homes there is no linen on the bed. Several members of the family sleep on the same bed or straw.[2]

The average rent is from eight to ten dollars. The housekeeper says the tenant is apt to let his rent "go," when he has

---

[1] Monograph viii.   [2] Monographs xv, xix, xx.

resolved to move, as long as the landlord will let him. The tenant tells you that this is true, for this arrangement enables him to pay the deposit which is called for in taking new rooms. The rent is collected about the first of the month, usually by a paid agent. Sometimes the landlord himself comes to collect. He may take a lively interest in his tenants, securing work for them or helping them in other ways. The "Sheenie" landlords are said to have a more personal relation with their tenants, but "when they are mean, there is none so bad."[1] Not infrequently the rent is paid to the janitress or housekeeper directly. Sometimes she "begs off" for the family, thereby enabling them to stay another month, rent-free. The position of housekeeper is usually held by a woman, although husband and wife sometimes share the duties. The women dislike the "rough work," such as keeping the cellar and water-closets clean. Besides the general duties of keeping the house, halls, yard, etc., clean, she has to see that the house is "full." As a matter of fact, the housekeeper rarely cleans house except on rent-day. She usually knows little about the elementary rules of health save to "keep the dirt off her hair" when she sweeps. That is usually the most important consideration in the sweeping. The relation of the housekeeper to the family in the house is variable. Sometimes she is a vigilant friend in need and a peacemaker. Sometimes she "just lets things go." The housekeeper receives her rooms "rent free" as a bonus for her services. In general she is incompetent. Moreover, she has frequently a large family and is physically unfit for her duties. Occasionally, she will work, however, for better conditions. She may even complain to the tenement-house inspector or have a tenant write to the department. The following letters descriptive of houses in the neighborhood seem to refer to housekeepers of a different character:

"Dear Sir—Pleas and call at 511 and 513 West 44 Street whare the small poakes wear lat Spring the houses and hall are in a fearfel condison and the sinks the odor from them are verry bad and if not seen to i fear you will hat the same kase soon agan. Please and investigat the rooms are there are seven and eight

---
[1] Monograph vii.

children in too rooms which i think is great shame. See for yourself a the housekeeper sade she will not let the Board of Health enter in her housekeeping."[1]

"To the Board of Health:

Dear Sir—Please at this House there is not a bit of lith in the Halls at night and the tenants are afraid to spk for if th does the will be Put out see to it at once no gass top floor nor second floare the Will give no lith to us and all wood Fore Board if the hous is on fire afore you nor whare wee are and smoaking chimbles God help the Pooar the hav to Put up with a lot and has no lith too see what wee are goane."[2]

HABITS OF MOVING.

The tenants are nomads. They move from tenement to tenement, drifting from poorer to better quarters and back again according to the rises or falls in their fortunes. The average length of residence is about a year and a half. Sometimes the family moves from house to house in the same block or, again, they change to another district. The families who have lived down-town never move back again. Occasionally,[3] they move to a less congested quarter, to Harlem, for example. In several cases I knew of they bought a small house and lot on the instalment plan in New Jersey.[4]

I was interested in trying to find out the cause of moving. Sometimes the mother doesn't know herself. At other times, there is the desire for change; to live near a relative; to be in the same house with a friend; to have stationary tubs. The landlord does not suit; the housekeeper is cross to the children; the house is not kept in good repair; the neighborhood is going "to bad." The husband's work is in another part of the city, and the carfare is too great a drain on the family income.

On several occasions I went hunting with a mother, the better to understand the attitude of the movers. The mother just walks along the street until she sees a sign "Rooms To Let" or "Apartments for Rent." She does not like to consult an agent "because they never know what you want."[5] She looks at the vacant rooms,

---

1, 2 Report of Tenement-house Department, 1900.   3 Monograph xxiii.   4 Monographs xiii, xxiii.   5 Monograph xiv.

or rooms which are to be vacated shortly, in the most superficial way. Sometimes, to be sure, she wants the walls and woodwork painted or the cracks "stopped up."[1] That the rooms will be "swept" she takes for granted. Although the housekeeper rarely has the time or inclination to do any thorough house-cleaning for the new tenant. Then the woman pays the required deposit, usually half a month's rent in advance. She wants to move in as soon as possible. At home she tells the family that she has engaged new rooms. No questions are asked, it is all left to her.[2] Then comes the day of departure. The pictures have been taken down previously. If there is a carpet, it has been taken up by the father or son. The house is in a state of absolute confusion several days in advance. The father goes to the corner of Tenth avenue to hire the every ready van for two to two dollars fifty. Sometimes the coal man, the grocer, or a friend "in the business" does the moving for less. If the new rooms are across the street or on the same block, the furniture is "just taken over" after it has been taken apart.[3] Few trunks are used. The clothing is bundled into sackcloth bags or old sheets, into paper or wooden boxes. Frequently a neighbor lends her clothes basket. Some male relative "stays home to help along."[4] Most likely no repairs have been made in the new home—the kitchen sink still leaks, the stove won't bake, the window panes are still broken—and no cleaning has been done. The mother has not revisited the new rooms.

You have moved into your new home without having anybody enquire about your antecedents. Of course you must not have too many children—if you have, you must forget to mention some of them. "It aint your fault, you know, if you have got so many." Whatever your appearance the housekeeper will accept you, unless she is a housekeeper of one of "them new-fangled model tenements." You are not likely to move into those because you can not pay your rent weekly. The housekeeper is "too cranky" and you do not like the "crowd." The Forty-second street "crowd" is the worst of all, you would not be seen living there. You do not need a private toilet. There is more to clean

---

[1] Monograph iv. [2] Monograph xvii. [3] Monograph xx. [4] Monograph iv.

in the new kind of house. "You *must* use the fire-escape to put things on, and besides you want a place for your plants, if you have any." New tenements—"not much for me."[1]

HUSBAND AND WIFE.

Among the families I know the husband is the chief wage-earner. I found no cases of factory work among the married women, although several of them had been so employed before marriage. When the husband's work is "slack," when he is out of employment or chronically unable to work, or when he is a "loafer," the wife goes out to wash and scrub for seventy-five cents to a dollar a day.[2] This work of hers is irregular but it goes to pay the rent. The husband brings his wages to his wife at the end of the week or fortnight. He gives her the whole amount and receives back carfare and "beer" money;[3] or he gives her as much as "he feels like" or "as much as he has left after Saturday night." One man I know deposits the greater part of his earnings in the bank and puts the amount he thinks necessary for the household in the glass on the mantel.[4] Another man I know gave only spasmodically and was termed "mean" by his wife.[5] Sometimes the husband does not tell the wife the amount of his wages.[6] Usually he gives her money for his own insurance. The wife either pays for her own and the children's herself or "saves it" from the household money. One woman I know worked on "the sly" and had a secret "store"[7] under the mattress.[8] Her husband would "whip her if he knew."[9] Another woman "served" to make a few extra dollars. She used this money to buy herself dresses for the "rackets." When the girl was sufficiently "attachéd" she put her savings in the "bank book."[10]

One husband, a German, always tended to the "money matters and buying" himself. When he died his wife did not know "the first thing about how much it cost to bring up a family."[11]

The husband comes home at night, has his dinner, and goes out with the "men," or sits at home to read his paper. He does

---

[1] Monograph vii.   [2] Monographs xiv, xv, xx.   [3] Monograph xvii.   [4] Monograph vii.
[5] Monograph xix.   [6] Monographs xvii, xix.   [7] Monograph xviii.   [8] Monograph xviii.
[9] Monograph xviii.   [10] Monograph ii.   [11] Monograph xix.

not wish the companionship of his wife. She keeps house for him and bears his children. "And them as don't want 'em usually has 'em."[1] He does not ill-treat her unless he is a brute or habitually drunk, but there is little spiritual comradeship. He is too tired at night to be interested in her domestic trials. The husband does not help the wife in the duty of child-rearing. He does not heed her physical weariness. She just "has to have more children." One woman had to give up playing the violin because her husband thought it unnecessary.[2] There is little respect. They refer to each other as "Her" and "Him."[3] They do not hide their feelings when speaking of each other. Mothers warn their daughters not to marry, telling them that there are plenty of "chances" still to come and "you can always get married."[4] They speak of marriage as a necessary evil. They advise all young women to remain single if they wish to be happy. And yet it seems strange to them that a woman of twenty-three or five should be unmarried. Most of them are married at eighteen. "Few is the husbands that don't abuse you or get drunk, I never knew any."[5] "Saints and men who don't drink don't live on earth."[6] The wife has to stand plenty of cursing "and say nothing." At times she is "whipped" or "struck."[7] If he is "too full" she goes out.[8] One woman showed me a scar where her husband had "hit" her with an iron.[9] One man ran after his wife in order to stick hat pins through her. He had just come from the saloon. When living together becomes impossible, the one or the other "just goes off."[10] When "her man" said that he did not want to be bothered with her step child "she put him out for good."[11] "And there's no forgiving him if he comes back." Often, moreover, the quarrel is "patched up." I found several cases in which the husband and wife separated[12] and then lived[13] together again for a number of years. Even when a woman has separated from her husband for good reasons she is always "wishing him back." The men do not like "other men folks around." "It looks bad."

---

1 Monograph ii. 2 Monograph xvi. 3 Monograph xvii. 4, 5 Monograph vii.
6 Monograph xii. 7 Monograph xix. 8, 9 Monograph xv. 10 Monographs iv, xiv, xvii. 11 Monograph xvii 12, 13 In this case the wife calls herself "widder," to protect herself from her neighbor's gossip.

There are few cases of compatibility, although the choice of a mate is unhampered. The common opinion is nevertheless that "its just luck after all—what you strike." A young girl meets a young man. He becomes her "gentleman friend." "They keep company" for a short or long period. He "comes 'round" one night in the week. He takes her to the "thé-atre," to a "racket" or to Coney Island in summer. They exchange photographs in the shape of buttons, which they wear. Sometimes they exchange rings (this does not necessarily mean an engagement). They give each other Christmas gifts, a silk muffler, hand-made wrist warmers, a knitted silk necktie, a manicure set, a gold brooch,[1] cologne, etc.[2] "If he aint steady, he's dropped." He must not take another girl to a "show." The young people keep company on the stoop, sometimes the girl "brings him up,"[3] If he has a married brother or sister he takes her to see them.[4] While he starts in to "save," she begins a "box." The box includes sofa-pillows, tidies, etc.[5]

RELATIONS BETWEEN PARENTS AND CHILDREN.

The women remain at work up to confinement, and then return to the hard work of scrubbing or washing at the end of a fortnight.

During the day, when the mother is out at work the child is cared for indifferently by some member of the family, usually also a child or by a neighbor, or it is taken to a day nursery.

The child is nursed irregularly. When the mother "goes out for the day" she nurses the baby at meal-times and during the night. Irregular artificial feedings supplement her nursings. In the case of the non-wage-earning mother the nursings are equally irregular. The child is nursed when it cries or whenever the mother thinks it necessary. The clock is not consulted: When the milk does not agree the physician is not called in until the child is seriously ill. Nursing lasts from one month to sixteen or eighteen months. The Germans usually nurse their children about a year, but sometimes the nursing is continued by both German and Irish mothers for a period of two years because the mother believes that it hinders conception.

---

[1] Monographs ii, vii, xvii, xix.   [2] Monographs ii, vii, xvii, xix.   [3] Monograph xix.
[4] Monograph vii.   [5] Monograph xvii.

When the child is weaned during the first year, it is invariably badly fed during the second year, usually overfed. It gets "everything on the table" from fried pork to pie.[1] One mother gave her baby whiskey "to make her strong." The mothers rarely change the number of nursings as the child grows older. When they do so it is not a systematic change as from first to third or third to sixth month.

I never came across any cases of "wet nursing." "The mother does not want to nurse other people's babies" even when she has too much milk.[2] I never found a "charge baby" nursed by its foster mother. She invariably gives it the bottle.

The mother tries to bathe her new-born infant as regularly as possible, usually daily, if she finds time.[3] The tin or wooden bathtub is brought into the kitchen. I found cases where the mother did not know how to hold the child in the tub.

It is not a sweeping statement to say that none of the children get enough fresh air. The infant is taken out by the older sister for an "airing" or the mother takes the child with her if she goes "on an errand." There is no regularity about the outings. The babies do not get enough fresh air in the rooms, either. The mother is usually afraid of letting the window be open. In the bedroom the air is foul and putrescent. In one case the mother took her baby out on the coldest winter days. She did not understand why the child developed bronchitis.[4] In another case a mother whose child had the measles took her out at any rate.[5] More attention was given to this important need when the mother had been a nursemaid in an up-town family prior to her marriage.[6] Frequently the children are not sufficiently warmly clad. They have little underclothing. Some of the children who are sick during the summer are taken for a ride on the St. John's Guild Floating Hospital or spend a week at Sea Breeze[7] (the A. I. C. P. Home). (In the care of the older children the mother is equally untaught about the practical aspect of food values.)

The poor physical condition of the older children I attribute not so much to lack of food as to lack of a suitable dietary.

---

[1] Monographs vii, xxiii. [2] Monograph vii. [3] Monograph xxiii. [4] Monographs ii, xiv, xviii, xxiii. [5] Monograph xiv. [6] Monograph xxiii. [7] Monographs v, vii, xiii.

Ill-cooked cereals, fried meats and pickles, canned vegetables, condensed milk, do not develop bone and muscle. Sometimes the child goes to school without his breakfast because the mother is not up in time or because he has overslept. If the child were to wait for his breakfast he would be late to school and "teacher would send him home."[1]

Sometimes the child brought candy and pickles for lunch to save the trouble of cooking. When the mother goes out to work the child has frequently only such food as she could prepare before leaving. Sometimes the father cooks or the children themselves fry the pork chops.[2] Sometimes the lunch is cold and is bought at the delicatessen store. The supper is served at irregular times. The children eat the heavy suppers of the adults.[3] Frequently the marketing for the meal is not done until an hour or two in advance. The wife does not buy of her own free will; "she waits to hear what her man wants for his dinner."[4] At noon one sees the children go into the family entrance of the nearest saloon and come back with the foaming beer.[5] There is an enormous consumption of tea by all the members of the family. Sometimes it is drunk four times a day. It is prepared in the morning and stands all day. At various times hot water is poured on these same tea leaves. The "drink" is dark and muddy and undoubtedly poisonous.[6] Coffee is usually also of the "long-standing kind." Whiskey is taken occasionally and given to the children "to make them feel good,"[7] or "stop the colic."[8] Wine is given to all visitors during Christmas and New Year's week. The children drink vinegar "because sour things taste good."[9] Milk is purchased at the grocery store in tin pails by almost all the families I have known. It is cheaper than the quart bottle. In spring the milk bought in family pails costs only four cents a quart, in winter five cents. The bottled milk costs eight cents a quart. Sometimes condensed milk is used and also "given to baby," diluted in water. The cover is taken off the milk pail and the milk is exposed to bacterial contamination. There is entire ignorance about preserving

---

[1] Monograph xxi. [2] Monograph xv. [3] Monographs ii, x, xx. [4] Monographs ii, xvii.
[5] Monograph ii. [6] The nursing mother drinks this also. [7] Monograph xvi
[8] Monograph ii. [9] Monograph xvi.

the purity of milk. In a few cases "Straus milk" was used with success, but the mother complained that the winter depot (253 West Sixtieth street) was inconvenient and that they had no one to send for the daily supply. Approved methods of preparation were tried by some of the mothers. They were glad to have me teach them how to pasteurize or sterilize the milk, but it "took up too much time" to do it regularly.[1] The same irregularity exists in regard to the feeding and care of the older children as in the case of the infants, only to a much greater degree. The clothing of the children is often lamentably dirty, scant and thin. I found few cases in which the mother did any regular sewing or mending, although in one or two instances the mother made the children's clothes.[2] The children wear torn clothes and ragged underwear. When they are worn out the mother buys new ones. "They are cheaper than making them at home." Frequently the mother "gets clothes off the lady" for whom she works.[3]

The children play on the street or run errands with a thin shawl to keep them warm.[4] Their underclothes in some cases are almost lacking[5] and rarely washed. They usually wear a woolen shirt and drawers of some kind.

The mother rarely visits her children's schools. "The Sisters know all about teaching."[6] She keeps Annie home to mind the baby; to "wash up" or run errands.[7] She does not know enough to answer the postal card sent by the teacher in regard to absence.[8] She does not "bother" to write that the child has been kept home through illness.[9] When the child has been sick[10] or at home or in the hospital she does take him back to school if the school authorities do not send for him. When she needs the child's help she[11] sends her to school late, for she knows she will be "sent home by teacher." When the teacher asks to see her, she does not heed the summons.[12] She tries to evade the truant officer.[13] This is especially true, when the child is working instead of attending school.[14] The family need the child's wages. The father says that "he, too, worked when he was a mere boy."[15] He will "be laid

---

[1] Monographs x. xvii.   [2] Monographs ii, x.   [3] Monographs x, xii, xiv, xx.   [4] Monograph ii.   [5] Monographs xix, xx.   [6] Monograph ii.   [7] Monograph xxi.   [8] Monograph xix.   [9] Monograph xxi.   [10] Monograph xvii.   [11] Monograph xvi.   [12] Monograph xxi   [13] Monographs xv, xx.   [14] Monograph xvi.   [15] Monograph x.

on the shelf soon," so he expects his children to "do their duty by him."[1]

As regards the enforcement and observance of the Compulsory Education and Child Labor laws, the transgressions are sometimes due to ignorance; at times they are deliberate. One mother[2] saw no harm in the fact that her children frequently played "hookey." Her child of thirteen, who hardly knew how to read or write, worked at a dressmaker's instead of attending school. Through my efforts the girl received a scholarship in the Manhattan Trade School. For a long time her mother saw "no sense" in the "pasting trade" which she was learning. The mother needs wood,[3] so she asks Robert to pick up old boxes and chop them for her during school hours. "It saves buying." She bids him pick up pieces of coal from the railroad tracks and search the ash cans. The widowed mother can not pay the rent so she allows her twelve-year-old boy to work before and after school hours, and until late Saturday night.[4] One boy of ten got up at four in order to "carry out bread" for a baker on the East Side.[5] One boy works until late at night as errand boy in a grocery store. "He gets along in school and gives me a dollar and a half a week besides." "Sometimes he gets a 'tip' at the kitchen gate or a bit for supper."[6] "It does not harm him for he would be fooling away his time in the streets or bothering me and the children if he didn't work." To the objection that he works late Saturday night the mother says: "But he has all day Sunday to sleep in if he has a mind to."[7] In one family the girls of fourteen and twelve both were "minding" neighbors' babies for a dollar a week.[8] A child sat with a sick neighbor and nursed her all night through an attack of pneumonia.[9] One child rarely went to school because she had to "mind" a baby to help pay the rent. One child "cleaned up a' Saturday night," and every afternoon; for this she got twenty-five cents a week.[10] The child of eleven who runs errands for a dressmaker for a dollar and a half a week, the girl who tries to sell "sewing" machines for two dollars weekly, the girl of thirteen who gets four dollars a week at the Five and Ten Cent Store, where she is not required to show her working

---

[1] Monograph xiv.   [2] Monograph xiv.   [3] Monograph xiv.   [4] Monograph xvi.
[5] Monograph xvi.   [6] Monograph xvi.   [7] Monograph xvi.   [8] Monograph xv
[9] Monograph xv.   [10] Monograph xx.

papers,[1] and all this during the school day, is not protected by the child labor laws nor discovered by the overbusy truant officer.

There are instances, however, of interest on the part of the parents in their children's schooling.

One mother complained that her daughter learnt French in school, which "she'd never need in her life." This same woman, who had been to see a teacher about her son's backwardness, "heard his spelling words every evening."[2] A neighbor of hers gave her brother "no candy money" because he had not been promoted and called "shame on him."[3] She hopes to have her sister of thirteen go to high school.

One mother showed me maps her son had drawn in school.[4] She did not understand their nature, but she knew he "must be smart for to do that." Another mother kept Annie's "good tickets" and "kindergarten cards in the drawer."[5]

Once a mother asked me to give her small boy lessons in penmanship.[6] When another son had to go to work at fourteen, she told me how much she regretted that "he's grow up so ignorant and uneducated."[7]

One mother[8] wrote to me that she was not satisfied "to have Willie remain an elevator boy all his life." She asked my advice about having him continue to "learn something."

The mothers dislike their children to ask them questions. "Children shouldn't be so curious." "That ain't nothing for a child to know," "Mind your biz.," "Shut up," "Hold your maw,"[9] "Ask your teacher," are some of the mothers' answers to the child. I never heard a mother tell a child honestly that she herself did not know about a thing. She thinks that this would be inconsistent with the idea that "parents know everything." When a small boy tells his mother she "don't know any algebra," etc., the mother thinks it is time for him to leave school and "set about earning an honest living."[10] She does not see why "Willie's always reading, reading, instead of going out with the other boys or seeing some nice girls."

I found few cases in which the mother did any regular sewing

---

[1] Monograph xv. [2] Monograph x. [3] Monograph v. [4] Monograph xviii. [5] Monograph x.
[6] Monograph x. [7] Monograph x. [8] Monograph xvi. [9] Monograph v. [10] Monograph x.

or mending, although in one or two instances the mother made the children's clothes.[1]

The children wear torn clothes and ragged underwear. When they are worn out the mother buys new ones.[2] "They are cheaper than making them at home." Frequently the mother "gets clothes off the lady" for whom she works.[3]

RELATION TO KINSFOLK.

Blood kinship is a strong factor in the tenement-house dweller's life. When possible he goes to a relative for aid. The kinsman is notified if there is serious illness in the family. He must come to offer his services. Attendance at the funeral of even a distant cousin in his own carriage and a "wreath" is a matter of etiquette. The relative in Europe must remember joyful or sad occasions.[4] He must write letters of congratulation or condolence. He must send "Christmas money" to the children, etc. Although letters are not frequent, Christmas and Easter gifts are exchanged.[5] "The women-folks are expected to look after you during confinement; and to congratulate when the new member of the family arrives.[6] The child is named after the grandparents, uncles, aunts, cousins, etc.[7] If the relative is dead the Catholic will give his name only if another is added for good luck."[8] The old mother or father are supported by the sons and daughters. They are visited by them and the grandchildren or they live with them in rotation without paying board.[9] The grandmother makes her grandchildren's clothes,[10] buys them shoes and toys; nurses them in illness,[11] brings them beef soup and "does those things which only a grandmother can do." Thanksgiving and Christmas dinners are eaten in common. If the family can not attend they send their regrets.

The children visit their aunts or uncles on Sunday or they stay with them over night.[12] An aunt who lives out of town comes to "stop for an indefinite time."[13] A cousin comes to stay with her aunt if she is looking for work.[14] Or she comes there

---

[1] Monographs ii, x, xiii. [2] Monograph xxi. [3] Monographs xiii, xx. [4] Monographs x, xvi.
[5] Monograph x. [6] Monograph xxiii. [7] Monographs xiii, xiv, xvi. [8] Monographs i, ii, v, viii. [9] Monograph ii. [10] Monograph ii. [11] Monograph xvi. [12] Monograph x.
[13] Monograph xvii. [14] Monograph x.

to stay if she is sick. Later on her aunt willingly nurses her young husband, or helps her to take care of her "first baby."[1] Sometimes visits of kinsfolk are dreaded "because they are too curious." One woman who was in great distress herself "took in" a distant relative of one of her married cousins.[2] The "relations lend the money for rent, for communion and for funeral expenses.[3] Sometimes they go so far as to pay insurance.[4]

On the other hand, at times relations with the kinsfolk are very distant and strained or are not "kept up" because of misunderstandings or lack of sympathy. One woman said one brother was not "sociable to the others."[5] "Your rich folks don't want to be bothered with you and you're too poor yourself to claim them that's poorer." "When I had fine furniture and fancy clothes my folks come round often," said a woman who had refused to go to her well-to-do sisters for aid.[6] One man never wrote to his favorite sister because she married a man whom he didn't like.[7] One woman gave up visiting her only sister because the latter had failed to congratulate her when her baby was born.[8] When the sister died she did her utmost for the bereaved children. She goes over weekly to visit them in Jersey. One neighbor "gave up" her own sister-in-law because the latter had "the cheek" to charge for services during confinement.[9] "And she's the one that brought all my other children into the world free." One sister hadn't visited her sister on her wedding trip in New York because she was ashamed of "me poverty and all me children, as if that wasn't God's will."[10] Of course she was "dropped straight off." One resident preferred to take her last dress to the loan office rather than have a rich sister "cast it up at her forever after."[11]

MONOGRAPH NO. I. CHARLES FERRELL FAMILY. OBSERVED OCTOBER, 1900, TO MAY, 1901.

Charles Ferrell, Age 80. Gray hair; brown eyes; pale; tall; round-shouldered; asthma since 1860; stomach trouble, 1900; chronic diarrhœa; lame foot, 1885; steady drinker; irresponsible; slow.

---

[1] Monograph xxiii. [2] Monograph xiv. [3] Monograph vii. [4] Monograph xiv.
[5] Monograph x. [6] Monograph ii. [7] Monograph x. [8] Monographs ii, vii
[9] Monograph viii. [10] Monograph xvi. [11] Monograph xvii.

Harriet Thompson Ferrell, d. 1903.	Age 69.	Gray hair; hazel eyes; fair; heavy build; periodically acute rheumatism, Bright's disease since 1886; dizzy spells, 1901; superstitious; believed in second sight; fearful; friendly; dropped h's (Cockney accent).
Thomas Clifford,[1]	Age 47.	Brown hair; hazel eyes; fair; erysipelas 1900; intelligent; friendly.
Alfred Miller,[1]	Age 45.	
Eleanor,[1]	Age 42.	Black hair; hazel eyes; fair; bronchitis, 1900; shy and reticent.
Elizabeth Mary,[1]	Age 41.	Pneumonia and bronchitis 1901; animated; energetic and full of life.
Daughter, d. 1867.		In infancy, of pneumonia.
Henry William,	Age 36.	Black hair; brown eyes; dark; tall; scarlet fever in 1868; left him with slight deafness; alert.
Son, d. 1869.		In infancy; scarlet fever; abscess and whooping cough in quick succession; died in spasm.
George Richard,	Age 31.	Black eyes and hair; tall; stout; appendicitis, 1897; grip and lame back, 1901; sullen and unfriendly.
Arthur Edward,	Age 29.	Light brown hair and blue eyes; fair; injured foot, 1900; pleasant manners.
Grace Bailey, Charles's sister's daughter, adopted, 1893.	Age 18.	Blond; blue eyes, one of which has a cast; fair; slight; narrow-chested; stubborn and " 'rd to bring up."

Charles Ferrell was born near North Suffolk, England, in 1824. His home was not far from Yarmouth, and he speaks with pleasure of living in the vicinity of the Yarmouth bloaters. He spoke little of his family. It was his custom to plant seeds on St. Valentine's Day in memory of his father, "who was a pretty good sort of a father and always planted seeds on that day." His wife says that he attended school only a few years. His father's folks were carpenters, so he became a carpenter, too, and got a job in their "place." Later he took up the trade of paper hanging. Sometime previous to 1855 he married. He had one

[1] Married and living in his or her home.

child by this wife. On her death, about 1855, he married again. He has a brother living in Brooklyn. He has never spoken of any other relatives. His wife, Harriet, was born in London in 1835. She was christened in the Episcopal Church, but attended the Baptist Church. She attended private school there. Her mother came from "the Kent Country." Harriet visited her maternal grandparents there every summer. She does not remember when her parents died or the cause of their death. "It happened long ago." She had a brother who died years before from tuberculosis, at twenty-two, and a sister who died in 1898.

Charles knew Hafriet since she was thirteen years old. Two years after the marriage of Charles and Harriet, Thomas Clifford was born. In 1858 the family came to New York city. They moved to West Forty-fourth street near Ninth avenue. At this time this part of the city was not built up and many of the families had their own market gardens. Alfred Miller was born in 1859, Eleanor in 1862, and Elizabeth Mary in 1863. In 1867 a delicate girl was born and died within the year of pneumonia. In 1868 Henry William was born. In 1869 Harriet gave birth to a boy who lived only a few months. George Richard was born in 1873, and Arthur Edward in 1875.

In 1858 the family settled in West Forty-fourth street and Tenth avenue. They remained there until 1877 when they moved to West Forty-fifth street, where they lived in the same house ever since.[1]

Charles had worked in a carpenter shop until 1885, when he fell from a ladder. This left him "ailin' and lame." He did not work after that except to "fit a key" occasionally. Harriet said that "he never did much more than support himself." The surplus went for drink. Harriet was "housekeeper" after 1877. The rent was thirteen dollars and eight dollars per month on the rent were allowed her for her services. Occasionally she took in washing for a dollar a day. Thomas went into the "ornamention'" business, *i. e.,* japanning, at twelve years of age. In 1872 Henry William served an apprenticeship to a silversmith on Union Square, but in 1895 he took to his brother's trade. He

---

[1] They broke up the home after their mother's death, 1903.

works in the painting division of the factory. His wages are seven dollars a week. He rarely works more than six months during the year. Since 1901 George also has earned seven dollars a week "japanning engines and injectors." He and Arthur, who works at a trunk factory, helps support their parents. Arthur has always, with the exception of a few years when he worked in a dry-goods house, worked at the same trade. He frequently changes his place of employment. None of the sons have ever joined trade unions.

The children attended public school until about their twelfth year. Charles and Mary had been married in the Episcopal Church and their children had been baptized Episcopalians, and Charles had once been an active member. He discovered, however, that "the churches all want money" and that it was more satisfactory in all ways "to look direct to God" without the mediation of the church. Harriet at first went to an Episcopal church in West Forty-third street, but she "went over" to the Baptist faith later and took all the children with her to the Central Baptist Church in West Forty-second street.

In 1884 Thomas "got him a wife," a Scotchwoman, and moved to " 'arlem." He has worked at japanning for twenty-two years. He brought his two children to visit his mother frequently. Alfred married the same year. He was a brass finisher. Harriet never hears from him. In 1885 Eleanor married Archibald Carswell. She and her three children spend several afternoons a week with her mother. In 1890 Elizabeth married and went to Brooklyn, "so the girls was provided for." She has two daughters. In 1893 Harriet adopted Grace Bailey, her dead sister's daughter, who had been an inmate of the Hartford Orphan Asylum since her mother's death in 1886. She is treated "like a real sister" by the boys. She is known by the family name, otherwise "there would be talk and they would not know where she came from." Charles has never heard from his oldest son since he left England.

Harriet was very strict with her children. "No one ever had any cause to gossip about them." She took great interest in "bringing up" her grandchildren. She concealed the fact of her husband's intemperance.

MONOGRAPH NO. II. ADAM KELLY FAMILY. OBSERVED OCTOBER, 1903, TO MAY, 1904.

Adam Kelly,	Age 63.	Iron-gray hair; blue eyes; flabby face; crippled by rheumatism; Bright's disease; irascible; phlegmatic; intemperate; industrious; gruff in manner.
Mary Elizabeth O'Flaherty Kelly,		Brown hair; blue eyes; toothless; emaciated; hemorrhages; heart trouble; St. Vitus' dance; temperate; emotional; slovenly; lazy.
Loretta,		Light brown hair; blue eyes; well-formed; responsible; attractive; industrious; neat; "motherly."
Joseph Alexander, b. 1884. Lived only a few minutes.		
Hugh Vincent, b. 1887. d. 1888.		
Mary,	Age 16.	Brown hair; blue eyes; pale; emaciated; hunchback; intelligent; industrious; patient.
Mary Ann, b. 1890. d. 1895.		
Celia,	Age 12.	Brown hair; blue eyes; tall; not truthful; indolent.
Adelaide,	Age 11.	Brown hair; blue eyes; steals from mother and sisters; dirty; lazy.
Frances,	Age 7.	Light brown hair; blue eyes; robust; tomboy; lazy.
William, J. B.,	Age 5.	Flaxen hair; blue eyes; emaciated; "stricture"; chronic stomach trouble; bright; lovable.

Adam Kelly was born in Formanagh County, Ireland, about 1805. He married in 1830. He had seven children. Adam Jr., was born in 1832. A daughter, Mary Ann, named after her mother, was born in 1833 (Adam, Jr., has spoken little of his other brothers and sisters. He never told his wife when his parents died or what was the cause of their death). Adam,

Jr., went to school and acquired a taste for reading. He was brought up as a devout Catholic. After he left school he drove a wagon for a large whiskey distillery. He traveled in Ireland and Scotland. He still has a Scotch brogue and uses Scotch expressions. At twenty-three (1865) he came to the United States. He lived in Brooklyn with his uncle and aunt, a Mr. and Mrs. McAloy and a spinster aunt. The women were his mother's sisters. At first he was a driver. Then Mr. McAloy, a marble polisher, taught him his trade. In 1880 he was "keeping company" with Mary Elizabeth O'Flaherty.

Hugh Vincent O'Flaherty was born in Kings County, Ireland, about 1838, of "good old Irish stock." In 1858 he married Mary Elizabeth Hines. Mary Elizabeth Hines had been brought up by a grandaunt, who taught her to read and sew before she was seven. At seven she went to school. She had a good handwriting and was a "fine sewer." At seventeen, two weeks before her marriage, she left school. Her brother went to the United States in 1871. He changed his name from "Hines" to "Haines," "to make it more American." He married in 1861 and had twenty children, of whom only four "grew up." The money given Mrs. O'Flaherty at her marriage by her grandaunt was invested in a saloon, which Mr. O'Flaherty opened in a small town in Kings County, Ireland. They had eight children, Mary Elizabeth, Jr., born 1859, four children born in the next four years and dying in infancy, Hugh Vincent, Jr., who died at fifteen of pneumonia, James who was crushed by an elevator in a cigar factory in New York city at the age of fourteen, and Thomas born in 1869. In 1864 Hugh Vincent O'Flaherty sold out and came to New York city, leaving Mary Elizabeth, Jr., the only child then living, with her maternal grandaunt. Mary Elizabeth, Jr., remained in Ireland two years and then joined her parents in New York city, crossing "all by herself." In New York Hugh Vincent O'Flaherty again opened a saloon. It was situated in Broome street. The family lived over the store. The children often stayed downstairs and their food was often cooked with liquor because their father could not do without it. Mary Elizabeth went to school for about seven years. "She never was much for lessons." She has not written a letter

for over twenty years. When she was fourteen she helped in
the saloon. She never learned to sew or do housework or cooking.
Hugh Vincent O'Flaherty wanted his daughter to grow up "a lady."
She never associated with the Irish, but made friends among the
Germans and Jews. She "kept company" and had many "gentlemen
friends" besides. One evening in 1879 she went to a church fair
in Brooklyn and there met Adam Kelly. Soon after he came to
her father's saloon "for a drink." Her father did not want him
around. He considered him too old a man for his daughter to
marry, and he found out that he drank freely. Besides Mrs.
O'Flaherty considered "the Hines and O'Flaherty's better people
than hisn." At this time Hugh Vincent O'Flaherty was paying
a rent of $125 and making as much as $700 a week. "There
were plenty who would have been glad to marry Mary Elizabeth."
In 1880, however, in spite of the strong opposition of the family,
she and Adam Kelly were married. The members of both families
were present at the wedding. Adam was earning about $10
a week. He was treasurer of the Marble Polishers' Union. His
father-in-law persuaded him to give up his trade and help him
in the liquor business. Then Hugh Vincent O'Flaherty began
to be interested in horse-racing. He lost a great deal of money
and began to drink heavily. So Adam had to carry on most of
the business alone. Mrs. O'Flaherty began to sew for a dry-
goods store. Later she worked at another store and a shirt
factory.

On July 30, 1882, Mary Elizabeth gave birth to a girl. She
called her "Loretta," because it was a holy name she liked. She
nursed the child one year. Mary Elizabeth has never followed
regular hours in nursing. She nurses the children whenever
they cry or seem hungry by day or night. From 1883 to 1889
Mrs. O'Flaherty took charge of Loretta. On November 2, 1883,
Adam had a street fight and was cut in the neck. It was a great
shock to his wife, and when the following February a child was
born it lived only three minutes. She says the German midwife
"was not quick enough." "The baby's head stayed in too long."
Mrs. O'Flaherty baptized the infant in the emergency, and prayed
over the dead body, "so that its soul would be saved." She

named it Joseph Alexander, "after the holy Joseph himself," and Adam's uncle Alexander. Adam reproached his wife for the death of the child. "A dead child was worse than none." In 1886 another boy was born. His grandmother "stood" for him and called him Hugh Vincent. When he was fifteen months old he got a sunstroke, playing on the roof with a neighbor's child. He died within the week. A fourth child was born in 1887. He was "born blue." The family felt unhappy that the child was not christened. After that Mary Elizabeth took in a charge baby because she had milk for a time. Mary Elizabeth, 3d, was born October 8, 1888. A few weeks after the child's birth "the saloon was burnt out." The enforcement of the Raines Law and the $800 License Tax made the business unprofitable. That was the beginning of the "downhill luck." One day when Mamie was fifteen months old Mary Elizabeth left her in charge of Loretta, who had come to spend the day. Mamie fell out of Loretta's arms. They took her to the Hospital for the Ruptured and Crippled. She became a hunchback with a paralyzed side. In 1890 Annie was born. She was named after Adam's favorite sister "Mary Ann." Cecelia was born eleven months later. Just before the confinement the family moved from the lower East Side to Ninety-eighth street and Second avenue, where Adam rented a saloon. One day, in 1893, while Mary Elizabeth was visiting in Madison street her father who was home alone, told her he had spent a great deal of money "for drinks and betting," and in her presence he cut his throat with a razor. She attributes the delicate health of the child born on October 8, 1895, to the shock. In 1894 the family moved to Forty-sixth street and Eleventh avenue. Adam was in hopes of finding business there, and he rented the saloon on the northeast corner. On February 12, 1895, Anne was playing near the stove in the kitchen. Her dress caught fire and she was severely burned. Mary Elizabeth believes that the nurses at Roosevelt Hospital killed the child by giving her too much morphine. On May 20, 1897, Frances was born. Before she was a year old she fell down stairs. Her head is very large. William James was born on October 19, 1900, he was named William after William Jennings Bryan and James after her father's brother, a soldier in the British army. He was not christened until November 4, in spite of Mary Elizabeth's wishes. "Fifteen days was too long to wait." "If he had been christened sooner he would have grown more." One day when William was a year and a half old Mary Elizabeth left some lye in a cup on the kitchen table. She had just been making soap. William played with the cup and swallowed some of the lye. His mother gave him mustard and sent for a doctor. After this he lost his appetite and could not retain his food. His mother read of a doctor in Thirty-fifth street and went to consult him. He charged five dollars for the first visit. The second time he asked five dollars more for using the X-ray machine. Mary Elizabeth could not afford to go back to him. She then applied to St. Luke's Hospital. She was unwilling to leave the child there, however, for both she and Adam were sure the child would die if it stayed in the hospital. She made no further attempt to have Wliliam treated until October, 1903. Then he was no larger than a one-year-old baby. He got brandy until I put a stop to it. In November, at my suggestion, his mother began to take him regularly three times a week to the Nursery and Child's Hospital, and he then improved rapidly on a milk diet.

Before 1897 Adam went back to marble polishing, working at a shop at Forty-seventh street and the North River. He received three dollars a day, but was rarely employed more than four or five days in the week. In 1904 he was still at the same place, earning from twelve to fifteen dollars a week, according to the season.

Adam has been insured since 1890 in the Metropolitan Life Insurance Company, at a premium of fifteen cents a week. In 1900 he could not pay his dues so he received "paid-up policies." All the other members of the family, except Loretta, have been insured in the Metropolitan Company, at a weekly premium of ten cents. Loretta is paying ten cents a week for her own life insurance to the Prudential Company.

Loretta went to the parochial school near Madison street for five years, "because it is most important for a child to learn the prayers and the holy stories." Then she went to public school near Ninety-seventh street for a few months. After 1891 she stayed home and helped with the children. In 1896 she went to work at the Higgins' Carpet Factory (Forty-third street and Eleventh avenue). In 1903-4 she was receiving there from eight to ten dollars a week. In September, 1904, she took a position as general housemaid for twelve dollars a month. In November, 1901, Mamie was taken by a penny provident visitor to the Henrietta Industrial School. Celia went to the school of the Sacred Heart of Jesus when she was nine.

Mary Elizabeth regrets that she married so old a man as Adam, although "she gets along except when he drinks." She never wanted so many children, "but we women can not help it." She thinks it unjust of Adam to reproach her "about having so many girls and only one boy." She warns Loretta not to marry as early as she did, and to be more careful than she was in her choice. She is never tired of praising Loretta and she encourages her to teach the other children manners and "fine talk." She herself has no control over her children, although she threatens and whips them.

MONOGRAPH NO. III. JOHN McGOWAN FAMILY. OBSERVED NOVEMBER, 1903, TO MAY, 1904.

John McGowan,
   b. 1832.
   d. 1903.
White hair; brown eyes; blind, 1900; pale; suspicious; not fearful; taciturn; coarse and vulgar in speech; admires honesty; lazy.

Mary Williams McGowan, Age 70.
White hair; blue eyes; sallow; illiterate; superstitious; very religious; garrulous; good-natured; thrifty; friendly.

Son,
   b. 1852
   d. within the year.

Son,
   b. and d., 1853.

Kate,
   b. 1855.
   d. 1868.

Son,
   b. and d.

Son,
   b. and d.

Son,
   b. and d.

Mary Jane
McG. Desmoran,   Age 42.   (See Desmoran Monograph).

John, Jr.,   Age 38.   Brown hair; blue eyes; ruddy; not superstitious; well-informed; alert; generous; eager to improve; courteous.

Theresa,   Brown hair; blue eyes; always an invalid;
   b. 1866.   emaciated; dyspepsia; pneumonia, 1900; 1902,
   d. 1903.   tuberculosis; illiterate; fearful; incapable; unfriendly.

John McGowan was born in Ireland about 1832. He was one of fourteen children, two of whom died in infancy. He attended the government school for a few weeks. At seven he became a "farm hand." At nineteen he became a sailor. He visited England, Scotland and Holland on his voyages. Once he went to California and visited other seaports of America. He earned enough money to bring his mother, three brothers and three sisters to New York. About 1850 he became a laborer in New York city.

Patrick and Mary Williams lived in the south of Ireland. They had six children one of whom died in infancy. Mary, Jr., was born about 1835. She never went to school. Her mother died early and her father married again. Mary came to New York when she was fourteen. She "lived out" and "minded babies" for six dollars a month. One morning when she was walking on Sixth avenue she "fell in with McGowan." He seemed nice; took her to the theatre and they kept company. About 1851 they were married. They went to live in West Fifty-eighth street. Mary had nine or ten children. One son "would be fifty-two if he had lived through the first year." Another son was born in 1853. In 1855 Katie was born. She died in 1868. "Then there was Mike and Stephen and Pat, God knows I don't remember thim all, but they is blessed for they died young." Mary Jane was born in 1863. She was named after her mother and an aunt. John, Jr., was born in 1867 and Theresa in 1868. In 1876 the family were living in West Forty-sixth street. In 1883 they moved to West Forty-fifth street. They have remained on the block since then.

John worked at the docks after 1860. In 1899 he was working "on the Jersey railroad." Oftentimes he was out of a job and did not trouble about looking for a new one. Mary did washing for "private families" at a dollar a day. Two days of the week she cleaned an office in the neighborhood for a dollar a day.

Mary Jane and John, Jr., went to parochial school. Theresa was too delicate to go. When John, Jr., was twelve years old he started to work in the Fulton market. He has continued in the fish business. Mary Jane "lived out." In 1888 she married Cornelius Desmoran. Tessie has never been strong enough to work.

Mary had always "helped out" her daughter Mary Jane. She has given her clothes, washed for her, etc. In 1898 when the latter's husband deserted her, she took Mary and her children to her own home where they made ten people in three rooms. Mary Jane gave birth to Mary, 3d, there. John, Jr., had to support them all. When Mary and Cornelius "made up again," Mary kept little Mamie "for good." She is "bringing her up." Since 1903 Kate Desmoran has also lived with her grandmother. John, Jr., is his mother's pride. He is the best of sons and not at all like other boys. He brings her his earnings. She is proud of his learning. She would like him to go to church oftener, but she does not believe in forcing children to do anything.

John never had much in common with his children. He did not get along well with John, Jr. He was especially severe toward Tessie. The neighbors say that he "drove her out of her mind by dragging her home one night from a house which he did not like her to go to." He whipped her because he was "disgraced." Mary always took her child's part and petted and wept over her, "poor thing."

John became blind in 1900. After that he stayed at home and ceased to work. In November, 1903, he was run over by a wagon as he came home from the Manhattan Eye and Ear Hospital. It was the first time he had gone out alone; one of his grandchildren had always accompanied him. He was taken to Roosevelt Hospital. For two days the family were not notified. "They might of buried him in Potter's Field for all we knew," his wife said; "while I'm alive and can work I'll give him a fitting layout." The wake lasted two days. She ordered three coaches and two barouches for the family, and the church society of the Holy Name also sent representatives in two coaches and "cried over him." "Then they had mass for him and offered special prayers for his soul." Mary crosses herself and says "God rest his soul" when she speaks of him.

Mary regarded John as unimportant. He never asked her about "home matters." He left the discipline of the children to her. She sometimes "saved an extra penny" and did not trouble to tell him about it. She misses her "man," however, because he was at home so much "the last years." Even as a young man he did not do his full share toward bringing up his children. "But he was honest and did not drink." On the whole, he was a "good man," and she was glad to be able to give him a "fine funeral."

After her father's death Tessie became even more of an invalid. She died of "hasty consumption" in 1904. All the old friends and neighbors came to the wake. She was "dressed handsome and had plenty of flowers." There were seven coaches. The insurance money all went for the funerals, but the neighbors say that the undertaker even then had not been "all paid." Mary was dispossessed soon after and moved to a house in the same street, nearer Eleventh avenue.

John, Jr., began to "keep company" in 1892 with "an Irish gal who minded a baby for rich folks on Fifth avenue." Subsequently she went to "the ould country to visit her dying parents." John "kept himself private from the gals" till 1903. Since then he has kept company with a German girl who works at a soap factory. She sent his mother a box of soap as a Christmas greeting. John "brings her up" to see his mother.

72 FAMILY MONOGRAPHS

MONOGRAPH NO. IV. JAMES MULLIGAN FAMILY. OBSERVED OCTOBER, 1903, TO MAY, 1904.

James Mulligan,
  b. 1817.
  d. 1883.

Sarah Mulligan, Age 79. Gray hair; blind; emaciated; failing memory; "piles" since birth of first child; bedridden since 1893; superstitious; patient; kind.

Son,   Water on brain.
  b. 1845.
  d. 1853.

Daughter,
  b. 1843.
  d. 1851.

Mary,
  b. 1849.
  d. 1855.

Bernard, Age 54. Brown hair; blue eyes; tall; stooped; not strong; conscientious; sober; good son and brother.

John,
  b. 1851.
  d. 1890.

James Frank,   Brain trouble.
  b. 1854.
  d. 1903.

Charles,   Pneumonia.
  b. 1857.
  d. 1902.

Son,
  b. 1861.
  d. 1861.

Mary, Age 41. Brown hair; blue eyes; thin; narrow-chested; delicate; sympathetic.

Bernard McGloin, a native of Cavan County, Ireland, was born about 1775. He married early. He had eight children. All of them lived to maturity except one boy who died at seven years. Previous to his marriage he had studied medicine at Cavan. He gave it up because he found that "he could not use his knowledge for his own family." He opened a dry-goods store in Cavan. He had a brother who had studied law and a brother who was a printer and had his own printing establishment. His son, Bernard, Jr., went to school for a time, and then became clerk in the Maguire grocery store in Cavan. He "kept company" with Sarah Maguire, his employer's daughter, and about 1820 they were married. They had seven children. The two oldest children died in infancy. Sarah, Jr., was born in 1825. Three boys, Bernard, John and Terence, came next. Rosetta, the youngest, was known as the "Beauty of Cavan." Her portrait was painted at Enniskillen and became a family heirloom. At sixteen she was married. She died at the birth of her first child. Bernard had carried on his father's dry-goods store after the latter's death. His son Bernard helped him. When Bernard died, about 1833, his son sold out the old stock. John went to his uncle's printing shop and became an apprentice there. The widow McGloin taught school at the County Workhouse from 1833 to 1843. About 1843 she died. Her daughter Sarah says it was from overwork and exhaustion to pay the debts of her husband's funeral, "which was handsome enough for even a Maguire." Together the children paid "the funeral money" of their mother. Sarah, who had attended school from 1832 to 1837, took her mother's position as teacher. The work was difficult. There were several hundred poor children of all ages. After a twelfthmonth she gave it up in despair. Terence had left home at about twenty-six. He married and had five children. He had been sick for a long time "and died from the shock of his mother's death" about 1843. In 1843 Sarah was "keeping company" with James Mulligan.

James Mulligan was born about 1817, seven miles from Cavan. About 1842 he came to Cavan and was employed in the Workhouse where Sarah taught school. James and Sarah were married in 1844. Sarah married because she lived alone. If her mother had lived she says she never would have married.

After a few months James set sail for New York to prepare a home for his wife. In New York he was employed as a driver "who took people about to see the sights." In 1846 Bernard McGloin, who had lost all his money in "horse-racing and betting," left for New York, taking his sister Sarah with him. Sarah joined her husband and they lived in Leonard and Hudson streets. Sarah worked at millinery, although she had never learned the trade. "It came natural." She realized that she had "married down hill," even before the birth of her first child. The change from the healthy out-of-door life to the dark and narrow tenement quarters did not suit her. "It is a pity that them that crosses does not know what they are coming to." She was not well the winter before her first child was born (1843). She was utterly ignorant of what she ought to do. The child died in 1853 from "water on the brain." He was "all laid out with flowers and candles. The woman who watched said pretty words to him and wove them into rhymes. Then she howled. James was cross and made her stop by giving her punch in the kitchen." In 1845 a girl was born. In 1851 she took scarlet fever. While convalescing she played on the street, got a relapse and died within a few days. In 1849 Mary was born. She died in 1855. In 1850 Bernard was born. Bernard McGloin, who was then employed in a newspaper office and who visited the family very often, "stood for" his nephew. John was born in 1851, James in 1854 and Charles in 1857.

At this time the family were living in West Twenty-first street. In 1860 they moved to West Sixteenth street. James was employed as night watchman by the St. Francis Xavier College. Sarah opened a candy store, but "it had not paid," so she gave it up after a few months. After this she wanted her husband to start a grocery store. James was sure that a second-hand clothing store would be more profitable. He soon gew tired of the grocery store and Sarah carried on the business herself. At this time she received no help from her husband. He spent all he earned. In 1861 another child was born and died within the year. In May, 1863, Mary was born. "The child born in May and dedicated to the Holy Mother is especially lucky." About 1863 the family moved to West Fifty-first street near Tenth avenue, and for a time James and Sarah carried on a furniture store in the neighborhood. Sarah made mattresses and helped upholstering. James was not regular in supporting the family and Mary had to get along as best she could till the boys grew bigger.

Bernard went to the Brothers' School, in West Sixteenth street, when he was seven. Sarah never went to the school. She said they were so different from the schools in Ireland that she could not have understood if she had gone. Later Bernard attended the Catholic Academy till about 1866. He had hoped to go to St. Francis Xavier College, but he wanted to earn wages to help his mother. John and Frank also went to the Brothers' School at seven and the academy until they were sixteen. Charles went to the Brothers' School in 1864. "He was a scholar and passed a civil service examination." Mary went to public school for four years. Sarah was sick in 1874 so Mary had to stay at home and keep house. "It was too bad about her schooling, but then it is not so necessary for girls to know as much as men do."

About 1879 Sarah began to live apart from her husband. She says she had "stood enough from him." She advised everybody not to marry. (None of her children did marry.) The boys and Mary lived with her. James "kept off." She sent Mary " 'round for money a Saturday nights," but he rarely gave her much. He only "sent 'round money when his conscience smote him." As Mary and the boys grew older, Sarah felt "ashamed," so she no longer sent to her husband for money. She considered herself a "widow." When James died in Roosevelt Hospital, in 1883, she dressed the children in brown, hired a carriage and went to the funeral. "Like as not the neighbors thought as we was burying a cousin." "But I had to take the children 'cause he was their father." If she had known the kind of husband he would be and that he had "another woman what he went 'round with" she never would have married him.

In 1866 Bernard became an apprentice to a printer. He brings home his earnings to his mother. "He always was a good son, God bless him. I don't know where I should be without him." John was an ice driver for years at nine dollars a week, but he never worked steadily. "He was not strong and always got cold." At sixteen Frank became a cabinet maker. "He could make chairs, tables, picture frames and all the tinkering you can think of." Then in consequence of a fall he suffered from pains in his head and eyes so he could not work steadily. He sawed wood and did odd jobs. Charles worked as a shoemaker in a basement. Owing to the damp surroundings he "got the rheumatism." In 1875 he became an expressman. He was often out of work. Mary, Jr., kept house and went out whenever she could find a day's washing, for seventy-five cents to one dollar a day. In 1890 John "got the grippe. It settled on his stomach. He threw up his heart's blood" and died. His funeral was small. Only three cousins of his mother and a few friends attended it. "There was not much show or flowers." A mass was sung for his soul at St. Raphael's Church. Sarah said the rooms made her think of him so she moved to West Forty-fifth street, between Tenth and Eleventh avenues. The afternoon of the funeral Sarah fell on the ice on the street and broke one of her ribs. She was bedridden until 1893. Since 1895 she had not been out of bed. Charles continued to grow weaker and "stay home." He died in November, 1902, of pneumonia. In December, 1902, Frank was operated on his eyes at Roosevelt Hospital. The operation was unsuccessful. "Brain trouble" followed. He died January 9, 1903.

The funerals of Charles and Frank were so modest that "people did talk." Neither had been insured. Bernard and Sarah are paying a weekly premium of fifteen and ten cents in the Prudential Company.

Sarah had aged since her children's death. She has lost her sight. She pined until Mary and Bernard consented to move from "the house of death." The family live in West Thirty-ninth street, between Ninth and Tenth avenues, at present. A cousin boards with them. He pays about one dollar and fifty cents a week towards the rent.

MONOGRAPH NO. V. DAVID CARPENTER FAMILY. OBSERVED OCTOBER, 1902, TO MAY, 1904.

David Carpenter, b. 1840. d. 1900.   Blond; blue eyes; fair; chronic bronchitis; caught fever in Civil War from which he never recovered; 1900, tuberculosis; suspicious; never forgot that he was a Scotchman; taciturn; laconic, even to family.

Mary Carpenter, b. 1844. d. 1898.   Brown hair; blue eyes; heart trouble; liked to read; bright; optimistic; lovable.

Son, b. 1861. d. aged four months.

Daughter, 1873.

Mary, Jr., Age 30. Light brown hair; blue eyes; pale; slight; sickly child; chronic bronchitis; refined; easily discouraged; gentle; quiet manners; affectionate towards brothers and sisters.

Son, b. 1876. d. within the year.

David, Jr., Age 25. Light brown hair; blue eyes; fair; slight; round-shouldered; not very intelligent; had no great feeling of responsibility; very stubborn; jovial; full of fun; lazy at times.

Hannah, b. 1883. d. 1886.   Of diphtheria.

Julia, Age 17. Light brown hair; blue eyes; chronic bronchitis; tonsilitis, 1900; quinsy sore throat, 1903; frequent boils, 1904; stupid; never reads; disagreeable disposition; taciturn; fretful.

Emma, Age 13. Flaxen hair; blue eyes; measles at four; scarlet fever at seven; bright; ambitious; friendly; neat.

John, Age 10. Brown hair; one brown and one gray eye; scarlet fever and measles at four; wild; frequently "left back" in school.

Edward, Age 6. Light brown hair; blue eyes; frequent colds; pleurisy, 1903; grip, 1904; spinal meningitis, 1905; bright; friendly.

78   FAMILY MONOGRAPHS

David Carpenter was born in the north of Scotland in 1810. His father was Scotch, his mother Dutch. The children do not know positively how many children their grandfather had as their father disliked to speak of his family. There were probably three sons and a daughter. Of these David, Jr., was the youngest, born about 1840. The family came to America in 1846. David bought a boat and carried grain on the Great Lakes. The family lived on the boat. In 1856 David, Jr., helped his father on the boat. David, Jr., never spoke of the death of his parents or their age at death. About 1859 he began to be a "helper" on a canal boat.

Mary Curtis had been born on this same boat in 1844. Her father, the owner of the boat, was an Irishman. He had married a Frenchwoman. Mary had two sisters and an older brother. Her mother's family were all in France. She never knew anything about her father's relatives. Mary lived on the boat with the exception of a few months spent at school in New York city. She had been taught by her mother how to read and write.

In 1860 Mary Curtis married David. The young couple bought their own boat and carried coal on the Lakes. In 1861 her first child was born. Soon after David became a volunteer in the northern army. He was soon "taken with the fever." In 1873 the next child was born. Mary, Jr., was born in 1874. She was a sickly baby and "came by it" on her mother's side. A boy was born in 1876, and died the same year. In 1879 David, Jr., was born. Mary had been sickly after her marriage and had always been too weak to nurse the children. They were "bottle babies." They had been born on the water. In 1886 Hannah was born, in 1887 Julia, in 1890 Emma, in 1894 John and in 1898 Edward. About 1886 the doctor advised Mary to live on land. So the family moved to New York city and settled in West Forty-seventh street. David came home only a few times during the year. A few days after Edward's birth Mary died. The baby was cared for by a friend who had nursed the mother during her confinement.[1] Mary, Jr., took charge of the other children. In 1900 David developed tuberculosis, and his daughter Mary nursed

---
[1] Monograph xvii.

him. The hour of his death the kitchen clock stopped going. She has not wound it since. Then she took baby Edward home. In 1887 David, Jr., had begun to help his father on the boat. By 1896 he had entire charge of the boats. The income from the boats varied from twelve to twenty-five dollars a week, according to the "dull or active season." In 1902 the boats "struck rock." They were put on the market, but proved to be mere "drug." From June to December, 1903, David could find no work. In December, 1903, he procured work at the Consolidated Gas Company for two dollars and fifty cents a week. Soon he was raised to nine. He gives almost all his wages to his sister. In October, 1904, he became a letter-carrier at fifty dollars a month. During June and December, 1903, Mary went out to wash. She now washes twice a week for a dollar a day. Julia has worked in a trunk factory since 1900 for three dollars and fifty cents a week. Three dollars of this goes to the household. The rest she saves "for clothes." In May, 1905, she left her old place to work in a silk mill for three dollars a week. Emma goes to Public School No. 17. She helps Mary dust and wash the dishes. John and Edward earn pennies by selling old clothes. The whole family attends the Ascension Memorial Church in West Forty-third street, and the children are sent to Sunday-school there. David is insured in the Metropolitan Life Insurance Company at a premium of fifteen cents weekly. Mary, Emma, John and Edward in the same company at a premium of ten cents weekly. Mary puts the spare pennies into the Penny Provident Fund for Spring and Fall clothing, and for a reserve fund in case of illness. David goes his own way. He never consults his sister Mary. Mary insists that it ought not be necessary for her to help along by going out to wash. She says that David is "too particular about his jobs." The relations between Mary and Julia are strained. Julia refuses to take her sister's advice. She stays out at night after 10 P. M. and goes wherever she wants to on holidays. Sometimes the sisters do not speak to each other for a week. Emma obeyed formerly, but wants her own way now. John and Edward obey Mary as they would their mother. Their father's brother and sister-in-law live near and pay them frequent visits. Their mother's sisters in Brooklyn and Connecticut are also visited several times a year.

MONOGRAPH NO. VI. JACOB KIRGER FAMILY. OBSERVED OCTOBER, 1899, TO NOVEMBER, 1900.

Jacob Kirger, Age 56. Brown hair and eyes; dark; pale; inebriate; irresponsible; selfish; dependent; sluggish.

Marie Kirger,
d. aged 37.

Lizzie,
d. aged 35.

Tillie Kirger Richards, Age 34. Brown hair and eyes; sallow; 1899, grip; 1900, grip; headaches frequently, strong-willed; lively.

Son,
b. 1871.

Kate, Age 17. Light brown hair; blue eyes; sallow; 1898, pneumonia; 1899, neuralgia.

Jacob Kirger was born in Germany in 1848. In 1868 he married a neighbor. Four children were born in the next four years. In 1886 the family came to New York city. They moved to West Forty-fifth street. Their oldest son left them on their arrival and they have never heard from him since. At the end of the year Kate was born. The mother died soon after. Lizzie, Tillie and their brother went to parochial school. Later Tillie went to the Workingman's School (then in West Fifty-fourth street). The children also were sent to Sunday-school and church regularly. From 1892-99 Kate was sent to public school (in Forty-first street). Jacob never had a steady job. At first he was employed as a boiler cutter. Later he worked at a wheelwright's shop in West Forty-fourth street for nine dollars a week. He spent most of this on drink, so the children had to look out for themselves. His selfish habits made the home unendurable. Lizzie got tired of it and married about 1880. Kate visits her occasionally on Long Island. Tillie married about 1887. Her husband "led her a miserable life." She never spoke of his death or of the date of her second marriage to Thomas Richards, the son of an Irish grocer. The Richards lived with Jacob and took care of Kate. Jacob's second son went to sea in

1894. In 1899 Kate was kept home from school because Tillie went to work in the wool room at Higgins Carpet Factory, where her husband was employed for seven dollars and fifty cents a week. She also did extra scrubbing in the factory. Later Tillie had to give up the hard factory work, but went "out to wash" for a dollar a day while Kate kept house for her father, who always wanted his dinner cooked by her. Tillie did not dare to leave Kate at home alone with her drunken father, and yet until she was fourteen Kate used to sleep in the same bed with him.

MONOGRAPH NO. VII. JOHN O'NEILL FAMILY. OBSERVED OCTOBER, 1902, TO MAY, 1904.

Jacob Vollman,
 b. 1848.
 d. 1882.

Brown hair and eyes; hasty consumption, 1882; autocratic; "German temper"; spoke broken English; sober; kind-hearted.

John O'Neill,
 b. 1850.
 d. 1902.

Blond; blue eyes; tuberculosis, 1902; illiterate; Irish in his sympathies; irresponsible; bad-tempered; lazy.

Margaret S. Vollman-O'Neill, Age 54.

Grey hair; blue eyes; near-sighted; flabby face; stout; short; illiterate; superstitious; uses coarse language; rough manners; gossips; dis-social.

Boy, Vollman,
 b. 1873.
 d. 1874.

Boy, Vollman,
 b. 1875.
 d. 1875.

George Vollman,
 b. 1875.
 d. 1902.

Brown hair and eyes; pale; emaciated; rheumatism of heart and pleurisy, 1902; intelligent; responsible; good son; kind.

Lillie, V. H., Age 28.

Brown hair and eyes; good complexion; sickly at birth; chronic bronchitis; pleurisy, 1902; ignorant mother; proud; "uppish"; neat.

Margaret, Jr., Age 21.

Blond; one blue and one brown eye; broad-shouldered; protruding teeth and jaws; chronic bronchitis and "female trouble"; phlegmatic; kind-hearted; disrespectful; dis-social.

Girl,
 b. 1888.
 d. 1888.

Henry H.,   Age 26.   Blond; blue eyes; broad-shouldered; healthy; convivial; ambitious; economic.

Henry H., Jr.,   Age 2.   Blond; blue eyes; sore eyes at birth; whooping cough and measles, 1903; weak digestion; friendly.

Among the immigrants who came to New York in 1838 was one Pierre Simplon, a Frenchman. Sometime after his arrival he married a native of Alsace Lorraine. The children did not know their mother's maiden name. Neither parents spoke of relatives in Europe and as far as the children knew they never had any communication with them. A son, George, was born in 1838. In 1839 a daughter was born. In 1841 another daughter, Katherine, was born and on June 26, 1850 Margaret, who plays the chief part in the following monograph, was born. Margaret does not know whether or not any other children may have been born and died. The Simplons were Catholics and attended church regularly. Mr. Simplon spoke French and a very broken German. Mrs. Simplon spoke German only. The children spoke German to their mother and English to one another. The family lived in the fifties near Eleventh avenue. Margaret does not know what her father worked at. Mr. and Mrs. Simplon died in 1854, within a short time of each other. Margaret does not know the cause of their death. She remembers the death scene of her mother when the latter confided her to her older brother and sisters. The orphans moved to West Fiftieth street. Within the next few years, the oldest daughter married. Afterwards she rarely visited her brother and sisters. Katherine kept house. George paid her for his board and gave her an extra sum for clothing Margaret. Margaret was employed in taking ropes apart and making them into stuffing for mattresses. The mattresses were then sold at a good price as genuine "hair" mattresses. Margaret did not realize until long after that her employer was a "swindler." At twelve she mounted silver tinsel on window shades. Subsequently she was employed in a large chair factory in West Twenty-third street in caning chairs. In 1864 Kate married. George moved away. He never gave his sisters his address. Margaret no longer received any help from him.

Her relations with her sister, which had been very strained even before the latter's marriage, now became almost unbearable. Although she paid board she was compelled at night to clean rooms, wash dishes and mend clothes. She was berated both by her sister and brother-in-law. Later she had to take care of her sister's children when the latter went out for amusement. Margaret has forgotten Katherine's married name. "I tried to forget it and everything about her," she said. In 1872 she was "keeping company" with Jacob Vollmann.

Mr. and Mrs. Vollmann with their four-year-old son Jacob and three daughters came to America from Germany in 1853. In later years Jacob never mentioned in what part of Germany he was born or in what trade or business his father was employed. He knew that his father died soon after his arrival in New York. Jacob never spoke of any relatives, either paternal or maternal. Jacob's English was very "broken." He always spoke German to his mother. He never read the English newspaper. He went to work very early. He was employed by a large chandelier maker. Previous to his marriage his wife did not know his employment, although she heard him mention in later years that he was employed by Mitchell, Vance & Company (241 Tenth avenue). Mrs. Vollmann was a devout Lutheran and her son Jacob attended a Lutheran Sunday-school during childhood. When Jacob met Margaret Simplon he was living with his mother in West Fiftieth street. They had lived there a long time. Jacob often took Margaret to the theatre. One Monday evening in January, 1872, when he called for her, her sister refused to let her go. Words followed and Katherine struck Margaret across the cheek. Margaret left Katherine's home and on the following Thursday was married to Jacob Vollmann in a neighboring Lutheran church. She did not tell her brother George about her marriage. After her quarrel with Katherine she always tried to avoid her.

Jacob took Margaret to live with his mother in West Fifty-first street near Tenth avenue. His mother had opposed his marriage. She often reviled her daughter-in-law for what she called her "Irish origin," thereby probably referring to her

Catholicism. Margaret had known of this opposition previous to her marriage, but she was "so tired of shifting for herself" that "even a cross mother-in-law was better than an unnatural sister." In a few months the quarrels between the mother and daughter-in-law were so frequent that Margaret was ready to leave her husband unless "he put out the old one." After his mother left, Jacob frequently visited her and he continued to support her. But she never came to see her daughter-in-law. Margaret was not told what part of his earnings Jacob gave his mother and she never thought of asking him. He brought home "good wages." In 1873 Margaret and Jacob moved to West Thirty-fifth street and here the first child was born. He was sickly from birth. His mother nursed him, but her milk did not agree with him. He was baptized in the Lutheran Church. He died when he was twenty months old. Margaret did not call in a physician at the time and did not know the cause of his death. She did not "know enough then" to do so. The next year, 1874, another son was born. He died aged thirteen months. A son, George, was born April 1, 1875. In 1876 Lillie was born. She was christened Lillie by the Lutheran minister. Margaret was sorry she was not a boy because "boys were so much less trouble." In 1878 the family returned to live in Fiftieth street. In 1881 Jacob Vollmann took a severe cold and was not able to work for weeks. He retained a hacking cough. Tuberculosis set in. By this time the family was in a very bad way. There was no money coming to them except through an occasional day's washing by Margaret. The physician who lived in the neighborhood was a stranger and sent them a large bill for his services. Jacob died early in 1882. When he was on his deathbed George Simplon came in and declared that his sister should not come to him for "funeral money." He had only just got through burying Katherine's husband and never expected to see his money again. To meet the expenses of the "big" funeral (the undertaker's expenses were $71.00 and Jacob was not insured), Margaret had to sell the parlor carpet and raffle the clock which had been a wedding-gift from her mother-in-law. The latter was done very reluctantly, because it was unlucky to sell one's wedding-presents. Jacob was buried in the Lutheran cemetery. Later the family saved enough money to erect a monument. Margaret and the children visited his grave several times a year. Margaret had no picture of him. Margaret says Jacob might have been a worse husband to her. They quarrelled frequently because he wanted his own way. They did not spend Sundays or evenings together. He went out to his "mates." After Jacob's death Margaret moved to 535 West Forty-sixth street, where they lived until 1893. Margaret supported the family by taking in washing. After school hours Lillie used to help her mother "clean things up," but she was never taught to sew or mend. George delighted his mother by earning odd pennies from the neighbors. At the end of the year of mourning Margaret married John O'Neill.

John O'Neill was probably born in Troy, N. Y., in 1850. He never told his wife the nationality of his parents. His sympathies were always with the Irish. He had an older and younger brother. The oldest brother never agreed with John, and died in 1901 without a reconciliation. With his younger brother John was on better terms. They "palled" together for a time when they were young. John never spoke of any relations. He never told his wife when his parents died. John was brought up a Catholic and desired his children to be brought up in the same faith. He and Margaret were married by a Catholic priest.

Margaret was not "roped in" by John with her "eyes closed," in spite of his promise to provide a home for her and the children. She had known him since she was fourteen. She had looked down upon him as the other girls and boys of the neighborhood did. She knew he was not steady at his work—he never remained anywhere for more than a few weeks—but she did not know that he drank and stayed out "until all hours."

On November 9, 1883, a daughter, Margaret, was born. A few months before John had gone off without making any explanation to his wife. She had to work hard at scrubbing and washing until a few days before her delivery. She says that because of this severe strain on her and John's bad habits the child was born with a weak constitution. Three weeks after the child was born Margaret had to go to work again. Margaret nursed the baby and, although the milk was not agreeable to her, she did not wean her for over two years. When John O'Neill came home he worked at odd jobs, as truck driver and iceman. Margaret never knew where he was employed or how much he earned. She knew that he spent most of his money on "drink" and that he was a "lounger." He never at any time contributed to the family support, and he never felt any responsibility even for his own child. He came home at night or not just as it suited him. His wife came to consider him "a bad man." At last in 1884, to avoid further quarrels, she drove him away. Although he came back several times with a promise "to do better by her," she was firm for three years. Then she let him come home. On January 15, 1888, another daughter was born. She died the following November. In 1889 John O'Neill left his wife of his own accord. He did not give any account of himself until 1898 and his wife passed as a "widder"[1] in the neighborhood.

Meanwhile in 1893 Margaret O'Neill moved to 610 West Forty-sixth street, securing the position of janitress there and thereby "getting her rent free." In 1889 her son, George, went to work as a piano polisher and by 1891 he was receiving nine dollars a week. He was paid bi-weekly and gave his mother seventeen dollars pay-day. Lillie went to work in 1891. She was employed at a French cleaning establishment in the neighborhood. She received four dollars and fifty cents for the first six months and five dollars after that. Half of her weekly wages she gave to her mother. The other half she spent on dress. "Lillie was always fond of wearing silk dresses and fine millinery." "Lillie was always a helpful child. She never answered back or gave me any sass." In the afternoon and sometimes at noon she had taken care of Margaret, Jr., when she was a baby. Lillie took Maggie to school when the latter was five years old.

From 1897 to 1901 Maggie was employed in different candy factories at about three dollars and fifty cents a week. Since 1901 she has worked in the same laundry that her sister worked in. Her wages are five dollars per week. She is often slack

---

[1] This is the usual subterfuge by which a deserted wife protects herself from neighbors' gossip.

or on half-time. Her mother is fond of her, but she has often whipped her as a "lazy lout." She is "made of bad stuff, like her father."

George and Lillie attended the Lutheran Church of the Redeemer (228 West Forty-fifth street) to which their father had taken them in his lifetime. Later they went to Sunday-school there as their father had wished. Maggie and her mother went to the Sacred Heart of Jesus (447 West Fifty-first street) two or three times a week. Maggie also went to Sunday-school there.

On February 2, 1898, after Margaret had succeeded in giving her children a tolerably comfortable home John O'Neill came back, only to make them miserable. He did not tell her where he had lived or bring her anything he might have saved. He felt himself the injured party. On February 5 he took the oath not to drink intoxicants, but he broke it on April 14. Margaret drove him away again. She hardly ever saw him again, although he sometimes came "like a beggar" to ask for a dime from Maggie, when he had seen his wife go around the corner. She did not think that she owed him any duties as a wife, because he had neglected to fulfil his duties as a husband. Whenever she gave him a few pennies, it was because he was the father of Maggie and the child they had buried together. Without his knowledge she was paying his life insurance premium (fifteen cents a week) to the Metropolitan Life Insurance Company. The father of her children should not end in Potter's Field. All the other members of the family have been insured in the same company at a weekly premium of ten cents.

In January, 1901, Lillie Vollmann, who was well liked by the boys of the neighborhood, was introduced by a mutual acquaintance to Henry Warrington. Warrington was an employee of the American Ice Company. He passed through Forty-sixth street three times a day, going to the foot of the street to get a new load. He had seen Lillie on her way to work.

Henry Warrington was born in New York city in 1879. He had four sisters and one brother. During his childhood his parents moved to Yonkers. Margaret had never asked Warrington about his father's birthplace or occupation or the time of his death. She had never spoken of these facts to her daughter. She said that these things were really not important and did not concern her. All Margaret knows about the Warringtons is that two of the sisters are old maids, "on the other side of forty;" one sister is married in the city, and the brother is married and lives in Yonkers, where he has a "nice little place of his own." The mother lives alternately with her daughter and sons. The family are Methodists and attend services regularly.

Margaret had put aside her savings for the past few years for Lillie when she married. Margaret knew "that things would come around all right." At any rate she thought women were better off if they did not marry at all, at least that was the result of her own experience. Margaret always permitted her daughters "to keep company if they wanted to." She never cared much about the matter. In the evening when the young men came "'round to the stoop" or even into the room she always slipped away to gossip with a neighbor. "Better to have young folks in the room than in a dark hall." In Warrington she was never especially interested, for, as she told her daughter, "there are plenty to be had." She knew, though, that Warrington had a "steady job."

In June, 1901, Lillie and Henry Warrington were married by the Methodist minister. Margaret did not like this, but as long as Lillie was a Lutheran and not a Catholic it did not much matter who married her. Lillie wore a blue silk dress and a white veil with orange blossoms. She had her picture taken as a bride. The young couple moved to Tenth avenue and Fiftieth street. Henry's mother lived with them for a few months and made things generally disagreeable. Subsequently she paid her daughter-in-law only occasional visits. Margaret does not know whether Henry helps support his mother. Margaret avoids her son-in-law when she can. She knows that he and her daughter quarrel sometimes, but "she shuts an eye and says nothing." During the current year, 1903-04, she has washed for her daughter Lillie every week. On June 20, 1902, Henry Warrington, Jr., was born. The child was born prematurely and was small and puny. At birth he was almost blind and suffered from sore eyes for the first few months. When he was nine months old he was weaned and "given everything that others eat." His grandmother, Margaret, makes his clothes for him.

In February, 1902, George Vollmann died of "rheumatism of the heart." His funeral was very elaborate, for he was his mother's favorite child. He had never given her one moment of sorrow. He was buried in the Lutheran cemetery next his father and two infant brothers. Margaret pays monthly visits to the grave. Every Easter she has flowers planted there. Some of the ivy from his grave she has brought home and set in a flower-pot. She has his last suit of clothes and his picture carefully put away.

John O'Neill came to George's wake. He was so changed that even his own wife did not know him. He had "hasty consumption." Margaret was too much bowed down with grief to refuse him admittance. Besides "all the neighbors were in and she wanted to keep up appearances." When John O'Neill saw the lighted candles and the coffin he wept and begged his wife to live with him again. Margaret said it was too late, but she promised to come to him when he was dying. He went away, persuaded by his daughter Maggie to apply for admission at Bellevue Hospital. He was transferred from Bellevue to the Manhattan Hospital.[1] When his wife and daughter were called to his bedside in April, 1902, they came too late for the end. Margaret did not grieve at his death. She was sorry that she had married him.

MONOGRAPH NO. VIII.   MARTIN O'BRIEN FAMILY.   OBSERVED MARCH, 1903, TO MAY, 1904.

Martin O'Brien, Age 53.	Red hair; blue eyes; fair; 1899, kidney trouble; 1904, rheumatism; stubborn; selfish; hard-hearted; drinking habits.
Bridget Donelly O'Brien,	Dark hair, eyes and complexion; stomach trouble; tumor and "female ailments," 1900, throat and nose trouble; superstitious; kind-hearted and grateful; easily discouraged.
John Donelly, b. 1884. d. 1885.	Pneumonia and tuberculosis.

[1] He registered as John O'Neill, 56 years old. Margaret could not understand why he described himself as four years older than he really was. He gave Margaret's name and the maiden name of his brother's wife as his nearest relatives.

James,
  b. 1885.
  d. a few months old.

Son,
  Stillborn, 1886.

Ellen,	Age 16.	Red hair; green eyes; freckled; small; thin; anæmic; swollen feet at ten months; 1901, measles; 1893, scarlet fever and pneumonia; 1894, grip and chronic bronchitis; stupid, bashful, stubborn, easily discouraged.
Martin,	Age 15.	Brown hair and eyes; dark; birth-mark on check (burned out leaving scar); 1892, scarlet fever and pneumonia; 1894, diphtheria; chronic bronchitis; conscientious; lovable; bashful.
John Patrick,	Age 13.	Red hair; green eyes; freckled; thin; tall; insomnia, asthma and bronchitis; ill-nourished; friendly.
Mary,	Age 11.	Brown hair; gray eyes; fair; thin; stomach trouble; 1900, erysipelas, chronic bronchitis; bright; friendly; affectionate.
Anne,	Age 8.	Red hair; brown eyes; small; thin; freckled; bones of head overlapped at birth; eyes did not open for three months; nervous and energetic; bright.
Thomas,	Age 6.	Brown hair and eyes, small, thin, delicate, chronic bronchitis; ill-nourished; bashful.

Bridget Donelly was born in County Tyrene, Province of Ulster, Ireland, in 1856. Her grandfather, Patrick Donelly, was a tall, stalwart, black-haired man. His people had lived on the same farm for generations. He married young and had fourteen children. Of these, nine died in infancy or youth. His first wife died and he married again. The second wife lived only a few months and he married a third time. The third wife bore one child. She was a harsh stepmother. The eldest daughter therefore left home and settled in Providence, R. I. Patrick, Jr., Bridget's father, followed her to the United States early in the forties. In 1849 he went to California for gold. After three hard years here and in Australia he returned to Ireland and married a neighbor, Mary Ann Hughes, the eldest of six sisters and one brother. Eight daughters and one son were born. Bridget, the third daughter, went to the National School in the parish until she was ten years old. Her mother taught her sewing and she helped in the housework. Her father died early; her brother John in 1875, aged seventeen, of tuberculosis, and her mother three years later. After her brother's death her mother was a prey to melancholia. She wandered around the countryside and was spoken of as "the crazy Widder Donelly." Bridget went to America in 1876. Through a factory agent she went to Gilbertville, Mass., to work in a silk and wool factory. The factory hands were French Canadians, Germans, Irish and native Americans. She lived in the house built for the unmarried women of the factory, she made a few friends. She attended the Catholic Church and sang in the choir. The other girls made fun of her. She admired and tried to imitate the refinement and the manners of the Gilberts, the owners of the mills. She sent all her earnings to her mother, not spending them on clothes as the other factory girls did. Thus her mother had been able to have a "decent burial." She likewise paid the passage of her two elder sisters, Nellie and Katie, to Gilbertville. Six months after Bridget left Ireland she was followed to Gilbertville by Martin O'Brien, a neighboring playmate and suitor.

Martin's father, Martin O'Brien, senior, was a well-to-do farmer. He bred, slaughtered and sold cows and sheep. Martin, Jr., had one younger sister and three younger brothers. When he left school he became his father's right-hand man and received a share in the farm profits. At his father's death his mother undertook the management of the farm with Martin's aid. She was left "homeless" because her rich neighbor, who lived in a castle, claimed the farm and land as his own. Then Martin decided to go to America to earn a living.

After he reached America, Martin O'Brien worked near Gilbertville at derrick-lifting and odd jobs. At first Bridget Donelly would not listen to him because she was working for her mother, and because she wanted to be sure that he would be able to support her. By 1883, however, both she and Martin had savings. They were married in New York city. Bridget had gone to New York by the advice of a maternal aunt whom she had visited from time to time in Providence.

Martin and Bridget began to keep house at 436 West Nineteenth street. After a year they moved to West Twenty-first street, and four years later to West Twenty-ninth street. Until 1891 Martin worked at odd jobs. Then he secured a permanent position as derrick-lifter, a position which he still holds. His wages vary from two to three dollars a day. After snow falls he has no work. He refuses to work at any other job. He belongs to the Derrick Men's Union and is a member of the Knights of Labor.

The first child was born in 1884. Bridget says that she knew nothing about the care of babies and that the child was not protected from dampness and cold. He died aged fourteen months from pneumonia followed by tuberculosis. Martin believes the boy would have lived had he not been named after his dead uncle, John Donelly. Another son was born in 1885. He was christened James at Martin's wish. He also lived only a few months. A third son was delivered still-born at seven months. Bridget attributes this accident to the quick succession in which he came to the dead child. Ellen was born in 1888. Her aunt Ellen, Bridget's favorite sister, stood for her. Bridget nursed her seven months. During the last three months of this period Bridget was pregnant and her milk disagreed with the child. Martin, Jr., was nursed for a year and a half by Bridget. Another son was born on November 25, 1891. At that time they had moved to Forty-fourth street. He also was christened John, but with the additional name of Patrick, after his maternal grandfather and great-grandfather, "to give him good luck." After John's birth Bridget developed a tumor on the side from which she still suffers. Mary Theresa was born November 12, 1893. Her aunt Theresa stood for her. Just before her confinement Bridget had moved to Forty-fifth street. Two years later Anne was born. Several weeks beforehand Bridget had gone to the office of a "swell" doctor, who lived off Fifth avenue and Forty-fifth street. She had to pay five dollars beforehand. She wanted "a pay doctor" who would do well by her. Owing to the physician's carelessness "the child's head-bones were driven together and the eyes had an extra skin over them." She was blind for three months. "The doctor never would have dared to treat rich folks that way." In 1897 Bridget took rooms nearer Tenth avenue. In 1898 Thomas was born. He was nursed a year. In 1901 she moved across the street. Several months later she took rooms nearer Eleventh avenue. In 1903 she moved to West Fifty-third street near Eleventh avenue.

Ellen and Martin had attended an industrial school in West Nineteenth street in 1893. Then they had been sent to two parochial schools. And still later Bridget sent them to public school after Ellen's confirmation. For this occasion Ellen had received a new white dress and veil. Her picture had been taken and "she looked grand." The other children attended parochial school and Sunday-school at St. Raphael's church. Bridget "hears their prayers" morning and evening. Bridget is "worried" because John does not know his catechism well enough to get confirmed. She scolds him for this, but she never goes to the school because she thinks the "Sisters do not want to be interfered with." Both Martin and Bridget are "regular" in their church attendance. Since 1903, with the exception of a few months' attendance at the Manhattan Trade School, from which she had received a scholarship through my efforts, Ellen has worked at the Higgins' Carpet Factory, for five dollars a week. Martin, Jr., also works there and brings home eight dollars a week. Bridget and Martin are insured in the Metropolitan Life Insurance Company, at a premium of fifteen cents a week, and the children at a premium of five cents a week. Bridget regrets that she had no preparation for city life. Martin had been compelled at times to ask his boss to advance his wages for the coming summer during the winter. The family lives from day to day.

Bridget says that you can not reason with "Irish stuff" like Martin, and besides that the wife always had to submit to her husband. She always refers to his "will," "a real O'Brien will" at that, she says. She married him because she knew "he had a good heart at the bottom." She rarely talks over things with him, because he is so strong-willed and gets so angry. Martin "stays at home nights." During the day when he is out of work or too drunk to work he "hangs 'round" at Murphy's saloon. But Bridget says she would stay with him even if he drank continually. However, she believes that poor people ought to stay single, as their life brings with it such insuperable hardships. If she had known anything about married life she would have remained single. Nine children are too many for any woman to bear. Six are too many to keep clothed and fed. But "it is God's will if he wants them to come or to go from us." Bridget is extremely emotional and demonstrative towards them. Oftentimes she threatens to whip them but she does not even rebuke them effectively. Once when Ellen refused to go back to the Manhattan Trade School Bridget "had a mad on" for several weeks and would not talk to her. She spoke of her as having "the O'Brien will" in her presence. She knew that from the beginning "there was no breaking of that will." She is just like her father, so she never tried to "break her will." Martin is tyrannical towards the children. He strikes them and acts roughly "when he is full," but Bridget is afraid to say anything. The children fear Martin, but mimic him in his absence. They do not ask "God to bless him" in their prayers.

Martin had not "kept up" with his brother and sister in Ireland. He heard that his brother married a rich girl "who brought her fortune along with her." His other brother, who is "well-off in Philadelphia," has "dropped him." Bridget also has a sister living there who is "high-toned." She never even came to see her on her honeymoon in New York, because she was poor, and had so many children. They met in Brooklyn in 1900, at the funeral of Bridget's favorite sister Ellen, but they "hardly spoke, and Bridget did not ask her over." Bridget's unmarried sister lives out as a cook. She comes to Bridget when she is sick and she is good to Ellen and invites her to "her house."

MONOGRAPH NO. IX. JOHN BURNETT FAMILY. OBSERVED OCTOBER, 1899, TO MAY, 1901.

John Burnett, Age 47. Black hair and eyes; overbearing; disbelieves in church going and in trade unions.

Mary Ann Wormly Burnett, Age 33. Brown hair; blue eyes (one eye closed); grip, 1900; illiterate; superstitious; feeling of responsibility toward family; talkative; friendly.

Daughter,
  b. 1893.
  d. in infancy.

Daughter,
  b. 1894.
  d. in infancy.

Daughter,
  b. 1895.
  d. in infancy.

Margaret, "Maggie," Age 8. Brown hair and eyes; fair; bronchitis, 1900; very disobedient; wild and bold.

Florence, Age 5. Brown hair; blue eyes.

Jane, Age 3.

John Burnett was born in Ireland in 1857. He was one of six children. The other five all live in Ireland. He hears from them occasionally. He married Mary Ann Wormly in 1892. Mary Ann was born in Leeds, England, in 1871. Her father died in 1882. About 1885 she and her mother (her mother's name was also Mary Ann) came to New York city. She had a cousin in Yonkers with whom she lived for a year. She also had a married sister in New York city, with whom her mother and she stayed until her marriage. She had a brother who was killed in the Spanish-American war. Her other sister she rarely speaks of. She thinks that her clothes are not good enough "to go to see her relatives. They would look down on her for being poor." After her marriage her mother lived with her until she died.

Within a year of her marriage a daughter was born. She died in infancy. In 1893 another girl was born; she also lived only a few months. The next year a third girl was born and died within the year. In 1897 Margaret was born; in 1900 Florence and in 1901 Jane.

John was a superintendent of free baths during the summer of 1898. He received eighteen dollars a month, with extra pay through tips. He was "put off" when "White Bill" came on. After that he held a position as overseer in a woodyard for twenty-five dollars a month. When he lost this position in 1899 he attended to "odd jobs" in a woodyard, receiving two dollars a day. In March, 1900, he was employed at the Fourteenth street subway for one dollar and seventy-five cents a day. Mary Ann has been a "housekeeper" since 1899, at a house in Forty-fifth street, between Tenth and Eleventh avenues. Before this the family lived in three other houses in West Forty-fifth street. As janitress she gets six dollars on her rent. The rent is seven dollars for two rooms.

John appears to be fond of the children, but he takes little interest in their bringing up. He never amuses them. Mary Ann is especially careful about the children. She never leaves them alone or permits them to play on the street. She bathes them every Saturday night and gives them clean underclothes. She likes to see them nicely dressed. She is anxious to give them "a good education." She also wishes them to grow up to be "good Catholics."

MONOGRAPH NO. X. HENRY HARTEL FAMILY. OBSERVED OCTOBER, 1902, TO MAY, 1904.

Henry Hartel,	Age 43.	Light brown hair and moustache; blue eyes; fair; slight; just; loyal; easy going; self-indulgent; good father.
Minnie Bopp Hartel,	Age 39.	Brown hair; blue and brown eye; reddish, coarse skin; very large and heavily built; family love and ambition for children; honest; very social.
William,	Age 19.	Brown hair; blue eyes; fair; slight; little muscular development; love for country and reading; easy going; impatient.
Henry, Jr.,	Age 17.	Brown hair and eyes; slight; narrow-chested; bright; conscientious, fastidious and playful.

Robert,
    b. 1889.
    d. 1890.

Annie,	Age 14.	Blond hair; blue eyes; stout; strong build; good-natured; helpful; phlegmatic; affectionate.
August,	Age 11.	Blond hair; blue eyes; fair; delicate; anæmic; bright; loyal; mischievous.
Rudolph, b. 1901. d. 1902.		

On the banks of the Neckar lies the little village of Wimpfen im Thal. It has a Catholic church and school. Further up is Wimpfen am Berg, which has a Protestant church but no school. At Wimpfen im Thal Henry Hartel was born in 1859. His grandfather and father Henry Hartel had lived there before him. For many years the latter was a mail carrier in Hesse Darmstadt. In 1857 he married a neighbor. A son, August, was born in 1858. Henry, Jr., followed, then two daughters and a son who died in infancy. Henry Hartel, Jr., went to school until he was fourteen. He went to the Protestant Sunday-school at Wimpfen am Berg. After leaving school Henry, Jr., was employed in box manufacturing. Soon after his father's death in 1880 Henry came to New York and took a position in William street in a box factory. He was followed by his sister Anna. Then came his mother and his other sister. They settled in Union Hill, N. J., where they still live.

The organist of the Protestant church at Wimpfen am Berg was one William Bopp, born in Wimpfen im Thal in 1827. He had married early. He owned a little farm. Of his fifteen children three died in infancy, two others before 1864, and four others when they were older. By trade he was a glazier, but he played the organ on Sundays and played the violin in the village orchestra on festival days. His daughter Minna was born in 1864. She went to the valley school until she was fourteen. She sang in the choir of the Lutheran church. In 1881 she left Wimpfen for New York city. Here she lived as general houseworker with a family on the lower West Side. As she was "green" she never asked for any privileges and seldom went out, but one evening she was visiting German friends and renewed her acquaintance with another visitor, her old school and choir mate, Henry Hartel. He took her home. At home he had always teased Minna, who despised him heartily and thought of him only as a bad boy. As a possible husband he was far from her thoughts. After this evening he did not see her again for a long time, but the courtship once begun was very short. After their betrothal they sent their pictures to their relatives. They were married in 1885. They moved to rooms in West Forty-sixth street. In 1886 a son was born. He was named after his maternal grandfather, William. (His grandfather sends him money every Christmas.) Henry did not like this name because Minna's oldest brother had died a short while before. Henry, Jr., was born in 1888. Several months before the family had moved to New Jersey because Henry had a job as a bookbinder in Newark. In 1889 they returned to New York, to West Forty-sixth street, between Tenth and Eleventh avenues, although Henry was still employed in Newark. Robert was born in 1889. He had a clubfoot. Minna thought he would be cured if she took him to Rhode Island,[1] but Robert did not improve there so she brought him back to West Forty-sixth street. She took him to the New York Society for the Relief of the Ruptured and Crippled. Not satisfied, she took him to the New York Orthopædic Hospital. After fourteen months he died. His mother thought it was best for him to die. He would have been a burden on the family. In 1892 Anna was born. Minna's sister Anna "stood for" her. She was nursed two years. In 1895, August, or "Gustave" as he is called, was born. His uncle August "stood for" him. In 1896 the family moved again to West Forty-sixth street, between Tenth and Eleventh avenues, where Minna was janitress. Henry's brother August boarded with them. In 1901 two days before her youngest child was born, Minna herself packed the family belongings and moved to Forty-sixth street and Eleventh avenue. She had saved a small sum in the Franklin Savings Bank for the newcomer and she engaged a physician a few weeks before to attend her. The child was christened Rudolph because his mother liked the name. He did not cry while he was being christened. "This was the reason he did not grow up." When Rudolph was thirteen months old he had convulsions one night

---

[1] She heard that there was a good hospital for cripples there.

and a few days later he died, according to the physician, of pneumonia.

Henry Hartel is an exceptionally steady worker, and more interested in his work than his neighbors. He remained at his bookbinder's job in Newark until September, 1903. He received twelve dollars a week in wages, five of this going to pay his monthly commutation ticket. He left his job then because he considered that his fare took too large a share of his earnings, From September to December, 1903, he was employed at a hatter's in West Forty-second street for ten dollars a week. In January work got slack. Henry made several attempts to answer newspaper advertisements but gave up soon. Then he sat at home in the kitchen and read the *Staats-Zeitung*. During this period he rarely "put on his shoes." In September, 1904, he went back to his work in Newark. Since 1900 Minna has been adding to the family income. In that year she took charge of a baby whose mother was in the hospital for eight dollars a month. In 1903 she took charge of an orphan whose mother she knew in Wimpfen. At first she received no recompense for taking charge of him. After he left in February, 1903, Minna took another charge baby for eight dollars a month.[1] She goes out washing at a dollar a day besides thrice weekly.

When William was seven years old his mother took him to public school. She brought him to school every morning and called for him at noon until he was nine. He graduated when he was thirteen and his framed diploma hangs on the wall of the living room. In 1900 he was working nine hours, six days in the week, at three dollars and seventy-five cents a week. In 1901 he was employed as an office boy for a trust company. Then he became a clerk at a cigar store at from four to five dollars a week. In January, 1904, he left this place because he saw "no chance of getting on." He did not tell his parents in the beginning that he had engaged himself as an apprentice at the Columbia Machine Works at four dollars a week. His ambition was to become a mechanical engineer. During the winter of 1901-1902 he went to night school for a course in mechanical drawing. He did not

---

[1] In June, 1905, he was adopted. Minna felt that she could not part with him.

continue in 1902-1903 because his work tired him. In June, 1905, he ran away to a farm in Vermont. He receives no wages for his hard work.

Henry, Jr., went to school when he was six and also graduated when he was thirteen. He went to high school for a few months, but soon gave it up; not liking to study. During the summer of 1901 he delivered parcels for a hatter. From November, 1901, to 1903, he was delivery boy for a butcher. His hours were from 8 A. M. to 7 P. M. On Saturday he worked till 11.30 P. M. He gave his wages of three dollars and fifty cents a week to his mother. Most of it went towards paying for his boots and clothes. In January, 1903, he became an office boy at a printer's at five dollars and fifty cents a week.

In 1896 Minna happened to hear of the Douglas Free Kindergarten in West Forty-third street, so she took three-year-old Annie there; and she herself joined the Mother's Club of the kindergarten. Annie stayed in the kindergarten for three years, then her mother took her to public school. From his third to his fifth year Gustave also went to the Douglas Free Kindergarten.

Henry has never paid any attention to the schooling of his children, except once when Henry, Jr., brought home a silver medal for proficiency in arithmetic. And although Henry wants his sons to enter skilled trades, he is doubtful about William's success. In June, 1905, he said that he knew "William would have a bad end." Minna shows a much more intelligent interest in her children's studies than her neighbors. She regrets that the older children did not have the advantage of a kindergarten training. She helped the children with the kindergarten songs at home. She tried to teach them German folk songs, but they did not wish to learn them. She has taught herself how to read and write in English, so the children will not "make fun of her." She insists upon regular attendance at school. She does not keep the children home to run errands, as the other mothers do. When they are sick she sends word to the school. She teaches the children to pray every evening. William was confirmed in 1899 and Henry in 1901, at St. Luke's, where they went to Sunday-school.

About 1900 a friend of William's took him to the Sunday afternoon Bible class, in the Baptist church, where "young Rockefeller teaches." The teacher there took an interest in him. She visited his home and helped him to obtain his position at the cigar factory. In 1902 they wanted to "rechristian him." Then his mother thought "he had better stop," although before this she had seen no objection to his attending the Sunday-school of two denominations. "It keeps the children off the street." She had never been in a Baptist church and knew nothing about Baptist doctrines.

There is less wasteful expenditure here than in any other family I know of. They spend less on alcoholic drink. Henry always has his "beer" for lunch and supper, but he does not buy or drink whiskey. Before the birth of a child Minna usually saves a little money. All the members of the family are insured in the Metropolitan Life Insurance Company—Henry and Anna at a premium of ten cents a week, the children at five cents.

Minna never leaves her children at night. If she goes out, Henry stays at home. The boys must come home by 10 P. M. They must tell her where they have been. On the other hand she has never sent the children to bed at a stated time. She waited "till they got sleepy." She does not think that you can teach a young child habits of regularity. You must wait until the baby "has sense." She thinks nothing of giving the children their heaviest meal at night.

MONOGRAPH NO. XI. GEORGE EVANS FAMILY. OBSERVED OCTOBER, 1902, TO MAY, 1903.[1]

George Evans,	Age 43	Reddish brown hair; blue eyes; fair. Steady drinker; delirium tremens, 1900; 1892 broken kneecap. Illiterate; hard; cruel.
Mary Fowler Evans,	Age 25	Black hair; blue eyes; fair. Reads, but writes very inaccurately and incoherently. Not superstitious; irresponsible.
Daughter, b. 1895. d. aged three months.		
George, Jr.,	Age 4	Brown hair; blue eyes; fair. At two years of age eye injured by a stick. More or less trouble since that.

---

[1] This family was referred to the Barnard College Penny Provident Collector by the C. O. S. district agent.

Edna,	Age 1	Small and delicate. 1899 bowel trouble; 1899 fell down stairs, fear of injury to spine; 1900 measles and whooping cough.

George Evans was born of Welsh-Irish parents, in 1858, in northern Ireland. He was the oldest of three children. He never went to school. He never referred to his father. He came to New York in 1894, with his mother and one sister.

Mary Fowler was born in Ireland in 1875. Some time previous to 1894 she came to New York with her mother and two brothers.

Mary went to live near Fiftieth street and Eleventh avenue with George Evans in 1894. She did not care for George, but her own home had been unhappy. She was willing to try "anything for the sake of a chance at a happier life." Their first child was born in 1895 and died after three months. In 1896 George, Jr., was born. Mary was not legally married until after the birth of this son. Then one of her brothers[1] insisted that a priest should perform the marriage ceremony.

From 1895 to 1897 George's sister had lived with them. Then Mary "put her out" on the ground that she was immoral. This sister had separated from her husband, and had placed two of her children in the New York Juvenile Asylum and the third in the Protestant Asylum in Peekskill.

George had worked steadily as a teamster previous to his marriage. The first three months of his marriage he brought home twelve dollars a week. After 1895 he worked "on and off" as expressman at woodyard, etc., for about three dollars a week. In June, 1898, Edna was born. George refused to work, so Mary's mother who had been living with them, took a position as chambermaid. She lost this and two subsequent positions because of her drinking habits. Mary's brother helped pay the rent when George and her mother Deborah both were "too drunk to work." Occasionally Mary herself went out to wash for seventy-five cents a day. In 1899 Mary had George arrested on the charge of non-support. She was unwilling "to slave for him" any longer. The court decided that he should pay his wife eight dollars a

---

[1] The brother disappeared in 1898

week and released him. Before this she had pawned all the family possessions. George had abused and maltreated her. He had gone out every night and she was afraid to ask him where he went. Then in 1900 he left her and went to live with another woman. She had him arrested again. He stated that the "other woman" had left him and he promised to take George, Jr., and support him and send Mary two dollars a week for the support of Edna. Mary did not mind not keeping George, Jr. She had always complained that he was "just like his father." Her mother, too, detested the boy and refused to help support him in an institution. Mary is fond of Edna and spoke with affection of the dead child "in Heaven free from care."

MONOGRAPH NO. XII. DANIEL McAULIFFE FAMILY. OBSERVED OCTOBER, 1900, TO MARCH, 1901.

Daniel McAuliffe, b. 1859. d. 1903. Black hair; brown moustache; became blind in left eye in 1898, right eye blue; fair; narrow-chested; unenergetic; despondent; died of tuberculosis; fond of playing cards; intemperate; took $25 from wife's drawer to buy liquor; never reads.

Theresa Ryan McAuliffe, Would not tell her age, "more than 35, less than 50." Brown hair, turning grey; brown eyes; pale; broad-shouldered; chronic asthma "in family;" gout, December, 1900; pain in heart and back, 1901, in Bellevue hospital; has been sick ever since her marriage; superstitious; religious; morose; headstrong; energetic; fond of dress and "finery"; vain; reads magazines and newspapers given to her; very kind and sociable to neighbors.

Helen, Age 15. Brown hair and eyes; wears spectacles; helpful; willing; bashful.

John Barnard, Age 13. Light brown hair; blue eyes; slender.

George, Age 6. Light brown hair; blue eyes; fair.

Daniel McAuliffe was born in the west of Ireland in 1859. His father died of tuberculosis soon after his birth. Daniel had four brothers and two sisters. One sister and two brothers died of tuberculosis early in life. Two children of a married brother as well as the oldest child of his married sister died of tuberculosis. Daniel came to New York about 1875. He boarded with two cousins who were dressmakers.

John Ryan, of Armagh County, married Theresa O'Neill about 1860. She had four brothers. John and Theresa had nine children. On the birth of her youngest daughter, Theresa, Jr., she died of asthma. Two boys died in childhood also of asthma. The father was so harsh in his treatment of his children that Theresa, a brother and sister came to New York about 1880.

Daniel McAuliffe met Theresa Ryan at his cousin's house where she was learning dressmaking. They were married in 1888 and moved to West Fourth street. In July, 1889, Helen was born. She was named for her mother's sister. In 1891 John was born. In this year the family moved to West Ninth street near Tenth avenue, where they lived four years. Daniel never had a "steady job" after his marriage. He was a hod carrier and driver and did "odd jobs" until 1892. Then "he worked on buildings." In 1894 he took a position as a driver of a delivery wagon at a dry-goods store. The family moved at the time to West Eighteenth street, to be near his work. In 1898 he lost the sight of his left eye in an accident and he ceased to be a wage-earner, with the exception of a few weeks' work in a stable in 1902. George was born in 1898. In this year the family moved to West Forty-fifth street. In 1898 "Tess" began to support the family by going out to wash and clean at a dollar a day. In the evening she did dressmaking for the neighbors. Besides this she made the children's clothes and did all the housework and cooking. "Nell" helps her in the house and runs errands for her. Frequently her mother keeps her from school to cook or take care of George. John began to sell papers after school when he was eleven. In 1903 Daniel died of tuberculosis.

Daniel felt no sense of responsibility for his family. He was willing to have Theresa support him. She worked "to the bone" for him when he was sick. Theresa says she was happier before she was married. Since then she has had nothing but "worriment." She says "not so many goils would get married if they knew what they were gettin' into." "You meet your fate and if you are to be happy, you will be happy. It is awful to be an old maid or widow. I'd rather take worriment than be that."

Tess has sent the children to the Holy Cross parochial school. She hopes that her daughter Helen will become a nun.

MONOGRAPH NO. XIII. WILLIAM LUTHER FAMILY. OBSERVED OCTOBER, 1900, TO MAY, 1901.

William Luther,	Age 42.	Dark brown hair and eyes; sallow; tuberculosis, 1899; lacks energy; quiet.
Maria Legen Luther,	Age 35.	Brown hair and eyes; fair; 1897 and 1900 two operations for tumor ("inherited from mother"); nervous; suspicious; irritable; proud; dependent; easily discouraged; spendthrifty.
Harold,	Age 6.	Blond; blue eyes; fair; 1900, whooping cough.
Ethel, b. August 1899. d. July 1900.		Blue eyes; fair; pneumonia; scarlet fever.
Theodore, b. July, 1900. d. within the same year.		Blue eyes; fair; frail; under-sized; sickly, did not digest food, fed on pasteurized milk; scrofula; marasmus; incipient tuberculosis of hip.

William Luther was born in Germany in 1861. His parents died in 1873. He was forced to leave school and go to work. He became a shoemaker's apprentice. In 1879 he came to New York city. He shifted round to various employments, but went back to his trade of shoemaker. He never spoke of any relatives.

Maria Legen was born in Darmstadt, Germany, in 1869. She was the youngest of three children. In 1870 her mother died. Her father was a drunkard. She attended school for "a year or two." She came to New York city in 1884, and went at once into domestic service.

Maria came over with her sister. They fell out over "money matters" when the latter married in 1896, and Maria has never seen her since then. She has not heard from her father or brother since she came to this country.

Maria met William Luther while she was boarding in a house in West Forty-fourth street with a shoemaker. They were married in 1896, in a German Lutheran church (Maria's family was Catholic, but she had never been devout. Neither she nor her husband go to church regularly). The Luthers moved to West Forty-fourth street, between Eighth and Ninth avenues (rent, thirteen dollars). After a year they moved to West Fifty-third street, and then in 1898 to West Forty-fifth street (rent from six to seven dollars).

Harold was born in 1897. In 1899 Ethel was born, and in 1900 Theodore. Ethel and Theodore both died in 1900.

William's work has been more or less irregular since his marriage; he ascribes it to the fact that there has been a decreasing demand for small shoemakers on account of the growth of the large shoe industries. In 1898 his earnings had decreased from twelve to nine dollars a week. In 1899 he got a position as a porter in a dry-goods house, where he averages ten dollars and fifty cents a week.

Maria pays two dollars a year for fire insurance. She has had William's and her own life insured since 1899 for ten cents a week each, on policies of one hundred and thirty-seven dollars and one hundred and sixty-eight dollars, respectively, in the Metropolitan Life Insurance Company. Harold is insured in the same company for five cents a week on a policy of one hundred and thirty-eight dollars to mature in forty-seven years.

Maria does not keep her home clean or neat. She makes all the children's clothes, however. She spends no money on clothes for herself. She has had only two calico wrappers since her marriage. As she rarely goes out, she says she does not need anything better. She considers it of primary importance never to fall behind in the payment of rent, and she pays cash for everything, but in 1900 she was twenty dollars in debt for Ethel's funeral expenses.

William has a strong sense of responsibility in regard to his duties towards his family. He spends his evenings, Sundays and holidays with them. He helps Maria clean the rooms and wash the dishes. He repairs torn shoes and broken furniture. He gives his wife all his earnings.

Harold sits on his father's knee every evening and tells him what has happened during the day. When the baby was restless at night his father would walk the floor with him. Both parents always speak German to the children.

Maria is devoted to the children and worries when they are not well. She was not able to nurse the baby, so she gave it cow's milk. The milk disagreed with the child and the mother was unhappy until the penny provident visitor suggested pasteurized milk. In 1901 she sent Harold to the Hartley House Kindergarten.

MONOGRAPH NO. XIV. HERMAN WUNDER FAMILY. OBSERVED JANUARY, 1903, TO MAY, 1904.

Herman Wunder,
b. 1861.
d. 1904.

Brown hair; blue eyes; bloated face; emaciated; tuberculosis; ignorant; inconsiderate; irresponsible; hard drinker; harsh; taciturn. Took last penny from wife for drink. Even asked children to beg for money. Told them it was not necessary for them to go to school; that they could get along better without it.

Anna Liebreich Wunder, Age 36.

Light brown hair; blue eyes; pale; flabby; healthy; washes until day before delivery; works short time after confinement; superstitious; poor memory; not religious; fond of exaggerating troubles; industrious; good-natured; affectionate, but harsh to children alternately.

Son,
b. 1889.
d. aged six months.

Nursed by mother whose milk did not agree with him. Mother does not know cause of his death. Never thought of having him treated.

Daughters, twins,
b. 1890.
d. aged 1 day.
d. aged 2 days.

Minnie, Age 13.

Light brown hair; blue eyes; anæmic; undeveloped; granulated eyelids; brain fever 1891; skin disease, 1896; scarlet fever, 1897; measles, 1904; appendicitis, May, 1905; stupid; very superstitious; self-willed; unenergetic; kindhearted; eager to help mother, but disrespectful to her.

Son, Still-born, 1902.		"Better for him because he would have had brain fever also." (Mother nursed Minnie until six months before his birth.)
Robert,	Age 11.	Dark brown hair; blue eyes; pale; skin disease, 1896; scarlet fever, 1897; stupid; unambitious; stubborn; disobedient; playful.
Frank, b. 1894. d. 1898.		Mother does not know cause of death; died in a hospital; mother never thought of asking nurse.
Marie,	Age 3.	Light brown hair; blue eyes; pale and ill-nourished; granulated eyelids; whooping cough, May, 1905; phlegmatic; bashful.
Elsa,	Age 1.	Light brown hair; blue eyes; granulated eyelids 1903; chicken-pox, 1904; measles; bronchitis; February, 1904, neighborhood doctor said she had rickets; child examined at Vanderbilt clinic, diagnosis proved incorrect; whooping cough, May, 1905.

Herman Wunder was born in Breslau, Germany, in 1861. His wife knows nothing about his parents. He had one brother who died of tuberculosis "years ago." She thinks that he still has two sisters in Breslau. He never spoke of any other relatives. He never talked of going to school, and in later years he never wrote letters or read. In 1887 he came to New York. His wife never asked him what he did before this.

Anna Liebreich was born in Wimpfen, Hesse Darmstadt, Germany, in 1868. Her father died when she was "too young to remember." Her mother then moved to her grandmother's home. She died a year or two later and left four children in the care of the grandmother. Anna says there were eight or nine children, but she remembers only six. "The others must have died." Anna's sister and brothers are still in Germany. Anna went irregularly to school, as she worked in the fields. She never reads or writes. Her mother's sister, Minnie, wrote to her from New York "to come over and get rich quick." Anna joined her aunt in 1885. On her arrival she took a position as general houseworker for eight dollars a month. In May, 1888, she met Herman Wunder. The following July they were married.

The Wunders settled in West Sixty-second street, and stayed there until 1890. Herman never had a "steady job." He worked in a gas factory or on the railroad near Forty-second street. He never told Anna what his wages were. He gave her whatever he liked and spent the rest on drink. Anna knew Herman had "the drink habit" before her marriage, but she was "lonesome and wanted to do what the other girls do." In 1889 a son was born. He died after six months. In 1890 Anna gave birth to "seven months'" twins, girls. One lived one day, the other two. Anna said: "It was better for twins to die."[1] Minnie was born in 1891. Her aunt Minnie "stood for her." Her mother nursed her only six months for Herman was not working so she had to go out to wash. She left the baby with her aunt Minnie during the day. Anna washed until the day before the next child was born in 1892. It was still-born. The next year Robert was born. By this time Anna was a physical wreck. She was hardly able to nurse the child. After a few months he was given "everything on the table" to eat. About this time the family moved to West Forty-fourth street, having moved several times in the preceding two years. Herman continued to loaf and Anna had to wash again until the birth of another boy in 1894. "His head was queer." He died in 1898. His mother thinks he must have had a sunstroke when he was a baby. In 1894 Anna moved to East Sixteenth street, so that she could place the children in a "home" while she went out to wash. Both Minnie and Robert contracted a contagious skin disease there and were sent to Randall's Island for treatment for a short time. By this time Herman frequently stayed away from home several days at a time. In 1895 the husband and wife separated, Herman taking upon himself the charge of Robert. Herman had been frequently violent and abusive so Anna was glad to get rid of him. Besides he never brought home "a red cent." She wishes that he had never "deceived her into marriage, for he brought her bad luck."

Herman ill-treated Robert. He took him out at night, letting him sleep in a saloon. Soon he grew tired of the child, and gave him to his aunt Minnie to keep.

---

[1] She could not explain why, she believed this.

Anna moved to 108th street near Tenth avenue, where she held a position as janitress. Here she got her rooms "rent free" and earned a dollar a day by washing. Part of this money she paid to the "Half Orphan Home," in which she had placed Minnie and Frank. In 1898 Herman found Anna out, but she refused even to see him. She considered herself a "widow." Frank had died and Minnie had been sent to Wimpfen to visit her great-grandmother. She remained there six months until the great-grandmother died. In 1900 Herman found Anna out again and begged to come back. This time she agreed and they moved to West Forty-sixth street. In 1901 Marie was born. In 1902 Anna separated from Herman again. She had very soon learned that he wanted to be supported. He was using her money "to drink himself dead." She said that she had enough to do to support herself and children. Nevertheless later in the same year Herman begged successfully to come back. In June, 1903, Elsa was born. Before this Anna had been too ill to work so through her penny provident visitor her rent was paid for a time.

Just before Elsa's birth Anna was advised by her penny provident visitor to send Marie to Randall's Island. The child was treated there for blepharitis and "consumption of the bones." She contracted scarlet fever there and was sent to North Brother's Island for two months.

Minnie went irregularly to Public School No. 51 from 1898 to 1902. Then, although she could barely read and write, she went to work as a peddler for a sewing machine company for a dollar a week, and later as a dressmaker's errand girl for the same pay. She frequently at this time had to work until 10 P. M. In September, 1903, she began to go to evening school, but broke down under the strain of the day and night work. The case was reported by the family's penny provident visitor to the Child Labor Committee and Minnie received a scholarship of two dollars a week on condition of her attending school for 150 consecutive days. This money went to paying the rent. In the spring of 1904 and again in the fall Minnie went to the Manhattan Trade School. She received another scholarship of two dollars a week.

In June, 1905, Minnie took a position as a book sewer for two dollars and fifty cents a week. Robert began to go to public school when he was eight. He frequently plays truant. His teacher offered to pay his carfare to Jersey if he would stay away, because he was "so bad." He works at a grocer's in the neighborhood both before and after school and until late Saturday night for two dollars a week.

In the fall of 1903 Herman succumbed to tuberculosis. He lay for weeks on his back unable to move. He stayed with the children while Anna went out to work. Finally he was taken to the Riverside Hospital on North Brother's Island. Anna said she was glad to have him taken away, but she visited him during the winter and brought him money for "tobacco and whiskey." Minnie and Robert had often derided their father for his neglect of their mother and them, but when he was sick they often went without food to bring him a few pennies. He died in April, 1904. Anna is not sorry that he died for he had brought her only misfortune. She gave him, however, a decent burial for her children's sake. Her aunt Minnie, who lives near her and has always been "like a mother to her," came in and "cleaned house" for the funeral. Anna had been paying Herman's insurance premium since 1900 until 1902, at first fifteen cents a week and later twenty-five cents. She felt that "he would go off any time with all his drinking."

MONOGRAPH NO. XV. THOMAS McKENNA FAMILY. OBSERVED NOVEMBER, 1903, TO MAY, 1904.

Thomas McKenna, Age 43. Black hair; blue eyes; pale; tuberculosis, 1903; Nephritis; erysipelas, 1903; since marriage often "goes off on tares"; comes home drunk.

Mary Elizabeth Black McKenna, Age 35. Brown hair; black eyes; bloated face; parts of body unnaturally swollen; miscarriage five months, 1899; hemorrhage of lungs, 1904; chronic heart pain and headaches; nose bleed, etc.; drinks frequently and heavily; calls it "feeling sick."

Mary Elizabeth, Jr., Age 15. Brown hair; gray eyes; fair; overgrown; lank.

Maggie,	Age 14.	Brown hair; gray eyes; pale; extremely thin; ill-nourished; delicate and sickly; headaches; sore eyes; sore leg.
Florence,	Age 11.	Brown hair; gray eyes; pale; ill-nourished; chronic bronchitis; stiff neck.

Son,
  b. 1898.
  d. aged one month.
		"Seven months' baby."

Son,
  b. 1900.
  d. aged three months.		

Thomas McKenna came from Scotland with his wife about 1855. He settled in Yonkers and worked at a pistol factory there. He had six children, two sons and four daughters. Two of the daughters died of tuberculosis before they were forty. Thomas, Jr., was born in 1861. He attended school irregularly from 1867 to 1874. In 1874 he was employed in the factory of the Eagle Pencil Company, Yonkers. Later he worked in a hat factory. When twenty-one he came to New York city. He was employed at Higgins' Carpet Factory, Forty-third street and Eleventh avenue.

Mary Elizabeth McCready came with her parents to New York from Ireland about 1831 when she was thirteen years old. She has spoken only of one sister to her children. The family moved to West Forty-fifth street. Mary Elizabeth never went to school in America, nor did she work before her marriage. When sixteen she married John Black, a neighbor. She was a Catholic, but John being a Presbyterian, they were married at a Presbyterian Church. In 1869 Mary Elizabeth, Jr., was born. She was christened in the Presbyterian faith. In 1870 John died of tuberculosis. Two months later a boy was born. He died of diphtheria aged three months. The widow wore "weeds" for two years and then in 1872 married Kane, a man of German parentage. His father had died early. His mother was at Bloomingdale Asylum for "light headedness." He had a brother who had also been "put away for being foolish." Mary Elizabeth, Jr., lived with her mother and stepfather. She does not remember whether there were any children before 1876. "Likely there was some though." In 1876 a son was born. He had "the Kane foolishness." In 1879 another son was born. He died in 1897 of hip disease due to his mother's carelessness during his infancy. Kane never had a "stidy job." His wife supported herself by washing. "He just stayed home." Mary Elizabeth, Jr., attended Public School No. 5 very irregularly from 1876 to 1882, and she went also very regularly to a Presbyterian Church to "learn religion." In 1882 she was employed at a wire factory in West Forty-sixth street at one dollar a week. From 1882 to 1888 she worked at Higgins' Carpet Factory. In the summer of 1888 "she went on a strike."

Thomas McKenna was also a striker. Mary and Thomas "kept company." In September, 1888, they were married at the First Presbyterian Church. This was "his'n" not "her'n." They took rooms in West Forty-third street. Then they moved to West Thirty-seventh street, and then back again to West Forty-third street. Since 1897 they have lived in three or four different places in West Forty-fifth street. Mary Elizabeth, 3d, was born October 2, 1889, "a seven-months' baby." On October, 1890, Maggie was born, also "a seven-months' baby." Maggie has been sick since birth. She was born with "boils." In 1894 she scalded her right leg by pouring the contents of a boiling kettle over herself. Florence was born May 5, 1893. Mary Elizabeth had been sick before the child's birth. She was a "nine-months' baby." Mary Elizabeth nursed her for about six months. In 1898 a son was born at seven months. He lived one month and three days. The next year Mary Elizabeth had a miscarriage of five months. In 1900 another son was born. Three months later he died.

Thomas was earning four dollars a week when he married. He is a piece worker at the Higgins' factory. He has frequently been "sacked" for staying away. He is frequently sick. He is also inefficient. Mary Elizabeth earns from one to two dollars weekly as a charwoman either "up-town" or for the neighbors. She never keeps "a job" any length of time. The McKenna family live from hand to mouth. No money is ever saved except for "insurance." Thomas and Mary have been insured since 1895 in the Metropolitan Insurance Company, at a premium of ten cents weekly, and the children have been insured since 1897, at a premium of five cents a week. To both Thomas and Mary Elizabeth school is not as important as "helping mother pay the rent." From 1896 to 1903 Lizzie attended Public School No. 51 irregularly. Then she left school because she thought of going to live with an aunt in Philadelphia. She did not go, but she stayed away from school two months. After that she was "ashamed to go back to teacher." Lizzie began to collect money for sewing machines for a dollar a week. Then she worked at a laundry in West Twenty-sixth street till eleven o'clock at night. Now she "minds" babies for fifty cents to a dollar a week. For a time she lived out because "it saved feeding," but she gave up that "place" because her mistress would not let her go to church. Maggie went to school from eight to ten. Since she was ten Mary Elizabeth has kept her home claiming that she was "too weak, and too handy 'round the house." In 1904 Mary Elizabeth promised me faithfully to send Maggie to school if I got her clothes. In 1905 the case was again reported to the truant officer. She also promised not "to give the new clothes away," as she calls pawning. Maggie attended school for about ten days, then her mother "sent her again to minding babies." She began to mind babies when she was ten years old. Florence went to school when she was ten.

Thomas and Mary are not often on good terms. Each one drinks secretly and tries to keep the fact from the other. Once Thomas was so intoxicated that he threw a flatiron at his wife. She still has a scar on her forehead. Husband and wife never go anywhere together. "My man has his friends and I have mine and they don't meet each other." Mary Elizabeth says she made a mistake in marrying. She would have been happier without a "man" who spends "his earnings on beer and the like." Then, too, she would have had "good clothes to wear to church." (As it is she never goes.)

Thomas and Mary Elizabeth feel very few parental obligations. They look to an early support from their children. "It is well to have as many children as you can because you have so much more money then." Still girls are a "bother." Mary Elizabeth believes in corporal punishment of the severest kind. The children think this is natural. She believes that you must send your children to Sunday-school "if you want the Lord to be with you," so the girls are given clothes 'a Sundays, which are invariably taken to "hock" 'a Monday. There is no regular hour for meals. The family do not sit down together. The children eat out of a "common bowl" ("it saves washing"). The usual diet is white or red cabbage salad, pork or sturgeon. The supper is "any old time." The quart of beer is never omitted. The children are usually in tatters. There is little cleanliness.

The family have little intercourse with any of their relatives except Mrs. Kane. Since 1903 she has lived in the same house with her daughter. She clothes her granddaughters and buys them Christmas goodies. Her two sisters live in Philadelphia. They have "come up in the world," so they have "little use" for her. A niece lives opposite and "comes in" occasionally. Thomas's brother keeps a "liquor store" in Yonkers. Thomas seldom sees him. He was notified, however, when his brother's oldest daughter died of tuberculosis, and he attended the funeral and sent a wreath. Thomas is on good terms with one sister. When he was sick she was notified, but she did not come to see him. "She would have come if he had died." Mary Elizabeth said she had never seen this sister-in-law and does not know her and where she lives. Thomas's other sister lives in East 118th street. Thomas never hears from her.

MONOGRAPH NO. XVI. WILLIAM HAERING FAMILY. OBSERVED NOVEMBER, 1903, TO MAY, 1904.

William Haering, b. 1860. d. 1902.	Blond; blue eyes; pale; tall; broad-shouldered; delicate from childhood; heart disease in family; died of apoplexy. Intelligent; ambitious. Strong-willed; self-indulgent; easily despondent.
Emma Seward Haering, Age 34.	Brown hair and eyes; pale; narrow-chested; 1892 operated for womb trouble; typhoid, 1900; chronic bronchitis; has internal trouble since birth of youngest child, 1899. Weak; vacillating; easily influenced; kind-hearted and grateful.

William, Jr.,	Age 13.	Black hair and eyes; dark complexion; robust; deceitful; disrespectful; untruthful; speaks English with German accent; self-indulgent; morose.
Therese,	Age 12.	Brown hair and eyes; pale; measles December, 1903; bright; ambitious; speaks broken English; fluent German; friendly.
Carl,	Age 10.	Brown hair and black eyes; olive complexion; measles December, 1903; operated for ear March, 1904; tonsilitis March, 1904; tonsils cut, 1904; speaks imperfect English; bright; inquisitive; affectionate.
Marie,	Age 9.	Blond; blue eyes; pale; measles December, 1903; dull; speaks little English; bashful; reticent.
Berthold,	Age 5.	Light brown hair; black eyes; pale; thin; measles December, 1903; speaks only German; affectionate.
Son, b. 1901. d. 1903.		Blue eyes; measles and pleuro-pneumonia December, 1903; ill-nourished.

In 1852 William Haering, Jr., was born in Mainz, Germany. He was one of six children. He went to a private school and later graduated from the gymnasium. His father then sent him to a technical school to study engineering. He belonged to a dramatic society and also to a fencing club. About 1876 he began to earn a small salary as an engineer in Mainz. Eager to advance he came to New York city in 1888. On the voyage he became acquainted with Emma Seward.

Early in the thirties, John Seward, with his wife and three sons, Thomas, Richard and Harry left England for New York city. They lived in West Thirty-seventh street. Dick was seven at the time. He attended public school until he was ten. Then he went into the liquor business with his father. When about twenty-four years of age, he started his own saloon. William was a colleague of his. The Burns's were Yankees who had come to New York city from "up state." Dick married Emma, the oldest daughter, in 1869. There was a younger daughter and several sons. Emma, Jr., was born in 1870. Florence, named for her mother's sister, came next. Emma died after Emma, Jr., was nine months old. After a few months of mourning Dick married his sister-in-law, Florence Burns. By her he had several children. She liked Emma better than her own children. Dick failed in business in 1880, and the family moved to Jersey soon after.

Emma attended public school from seven to fifteen. She began to study the violin when she was seven. Her father wanted her to be a "lady" and not to work. She never learned to sew or do housework. In 1886 she was sent abroad to Frankfort to study music. Before that she had been giving violin lessons and playing at private parties. In 1888 she was so homesick that she decided to return to America.

William Haering followed up his ship acquaintance with Emma. Within the year he asked her to marry him. Dick Seward forbade his daughter to see William. Then the couple eloped and were married by an alderman. Emma's father refused ever to see her again, although she wrote to him after the birth of her first child. In 1894 her father died. Her one sister "stuck to her" and paid her secret visits.

William tried unsuccessfully to find work as an engineer. At last he had to accept a job in a gas factory, "a big come-down." He worked there for the next eight years at wages varying from nine to twelve dollars a week. In September, 1890, William, Jr., was born. Emma says she did not know the first thing about children. The baby was sickly; he was nursed irregularly. In 1891 Therese was born. She was fed on cow's milk. She was named for her father's mother and sister. The aunt sends her niece one dollar at Christmas. After the birth of this child Emma had serious womb trouble. She "did not know enough to have it treated." In 1894 Carl was born, and in 1895, Marie. In 1897 the family moved to New Rochelle. Before this they had lived in various places on the West Side between Fortieth and Fifty-second streets. They moved to New Rochelle because William had read that there was work there for engineers. In 1899 they returned to New York city to West Forty-sixth street, and the following year they went to Mainz. William insisted upon going because he wanted to return to his old work. In Mainz he earned fifteen dollars a week. In 1900 Berthold was born. Berthold was the maiden name of William's mother. In 1902 another son was born. Emma had difficulty in nursing him. William began to suffer from acute heart trouble. He died in May, 1903. He had not saved; "Man muss seinem Stande nach leben," he said. Emma also refused to economize and insisted upon "keeping up appearances." Frequently during the period of their father's illness the children starved. Some of their furniture was sold to cover the funeral expenses. In July, 1903, Emma returned with her children to New York. She had announced her coming to her stepmother, and the latter met her on the dock. Emma lived with her stepmother in Jersey for a few weeks, then she went to West Forty-sixth street as her stepmother could not stand the noise of the children. In December, 1903, the baby died. Emma's father-in-law sends her eighty-eight dollars every three months. At one time she got work as "help" in the West Side neighborhood nursery at two dollars a week. At another time she earned fifteen dollars playing in two church concerts.

In March, 1904, her son William began to earn three dollars a week at a baker's. In July he got a position as elevator boy for fifteen dollars a month. Carl works after school hours and all day Saturday at a near-by grocer's for about two dollars and a half a week. When Emma's money gives out she pawns her clothes, violin, bed linen, etc., going from one "money shark" to another. During March and April, 1904, she received help in groceries from the Association for Improving the Condition of the Poor.

Emma says that her married life was thoroughly unhappy. There was "no luck in it," because her marriage was not blessed by her parents. William made her miserable by having everything his own way. He began by "driving" her to be a Catholic. She added, however, "I have found comfort in it ever since." "If you marry a man you marry his religion, too." William had "German ideas" about a wife's subjection. Frequently he did not speak to Emma for several days at a time. Sometimes he had "fits." Then he was so violent that she was forced to run away from him. He was gentle when she was not well and brought her flowers. In May, 1904, she sent money to Germany to decorate his grave. She says that she would not marry again.

Emma promised her husband to bring up the children "in the church." She therefore sends them to the parochial school. William, Jr., did not go to school until he was ten. In Mainz the children went to a pay school. Emma herself does not go to church regularly, but she is strict about sending the children to the Sunday-school of the Church of the Assumption. William was confirmed in May, 1904. His mother spent ten dollars for a new suit, etc., for the occasion. His sister Therese was his "bride," and also wore new clothes. He had to be silent and fast a whole day. Except Therese the children had no godparents. In her case the priest had insisted upon calling in a servant. Emma thinks this was "a disgrace to the family." William was always stern with the children, never hesitating to whip them. Emma always "spoiled" them. She "can not manage them" for they "run all over" her. They worry her night and day and wear her out with their quarrels. In September, 1904, she placed the two girls in a "home." In June, 1905, she "packed up" for a town in Vermont. She expects to give violin lessons there.

MONOGRAPH NO. XVII. ALEXANDER GREEN FAMILY. OBSERVED OCTOBER, 1902, TO MAY, 1904.

Alexander Maximilian Green, Age 42. Brown hair; blue eyes; broad-shouldered; lacks several fingers on right hand; tendency to tuberculosis; cough; drunkard; violent temper; insanely jealous; arrogant.

Ella Morse Lloyd, Green, Age 42. Gray hair; blue eyes; pale; careworn; prominent cheek bones; stooped shoulders; tendency to tuberculosis; chronic rheumatism; kidney and womb trouble; shrewd; tolerant; kind; tendency to oppose; good business manager; frugal.

Son,
b. 1883, Still-born.

Lula Lloyd, Age 20. Blond; blue eyes; short-sighted; impediment in her speech; anæmic; chronic bronchitis; "female troubles"; ulcers; nervous; tendency to untruthfulness; lazy.

Maude Lloyd,
   b. 1886.
   d. 1887.

Son, Lloyd,
   b. 1887.
   d. 1887.

Son, Green,
   b. 1893.
   d. at birth.

Son, Green,
   b. 1894.
   d. after few weeks.

Elizabeth Rosanna, Age 7. Blond; blue eyes; chronic granulations; fair; prominent forehead; delicate; rheumatic catarrh of stomach; parenchymatous keratitos, 1903; bright; obstinate; lovable.

Twenty miles from Rochester, N. Y., there is a small town called Brockport. During the seventies it had several large iron factories. Since then the iron manufactures have moved to the large cities and Brockport has lost, with its industrial prosperity, a large number of its inhabitants.

In Brockport the great-grandfather, grandfather and father of John Lloyd lived. John Lloyd was born here in 1853. His childhood was very happy. His parents' friends were the few neighbors whom they had known from childhood. His father insisted on regular attendance at the Methodist church and Sunday-school. He and his two sisters were brought up to be tolerant to all sects but Catholics. They were told that Catholics were thoroughly irresponsible and bad. John attended district school from 1859 to 1866, then he became an apprentice in an iron factory. He worked on mowing machines and became an efficient ironmonger. His father was very proud of him. About 1875 his mother died and his sister Bessie went to Addison, N. Y., to live.

So greatly was John attached to Bessie that he visited her several times at Addison during the following three years.

Among the immigrants to America from Germany about 1850 were a Doctor and Mrs. Green. The young couple had just been married before leaving for America. Soon after his arrival Dr. Green went to Yonkers and established himself there as a physician. Their first child was born within the year. He died in infancy of tuberculosis. Before his birth, Mrs. Green, herself, suffered from incipient tuberculosis. Dr. Green died in 1867, he left three children, Alexander Maximilian, who was born November 2, 1862, an older son and daughter. Constantly ill and worn-out with hard work, Mrs. Green died in 1875 of tuberculosis. At her death the elder son began to shift for himself. Georgina, the daughter, was placed in a Protestant Home in New York city, and Alexander left the school, which he had attended irregularly, and got a position in the factory of the Eagle Pencil Company, in Yonkers. Almost ten years later we find him doing odd jobs in Rochester. Previous to that he had been in Brockport, N. Y., and had traveled far and wide in the East and West. His adventurous spirit had even led him to Europe. He never saved any money, always working his way from day to day. Even now in later life he can not stay at a job any length of time.

On September 26, 1862, Ella Frances Morse was born in a small town in central Ohio. Her parents, Charles and Elizabeth Morse, were also born there. Ella was the third child. The two older children had died in infancy. In 1886 the Morses moved to Starklin, N. Y., a small village remote from a railroad station and surrounded by farmlands. Ella's father was the driver of the village hotel stage. Ella's mother was always a consumptive invalid, taking no part in the household administration. To the father the children had to go for everything, but so severe was he that rather than go to him they grew up by themselves. In 1874 the family moved to Shannon Corners, N. Y., a few miles from Starklin. Shannon Corners and Starklin both had a district school, which Ella attended. Again in 1875 the family moved to Addison, N. Y. Addison was a town of about two thousand inhabitants, consisting chiefly of Yankees and Irish.

Mr. Morse bought a farm on which he cultivated market fruits and vegetables. He also raised sheep and oxen, which he slaughtered himself and sold to wholesale dealers. Ella Frances attended one of the four district schools of Addison for one year. She remembers many school and Sunday-school picnics in the early Spring and Summer, and her great delight in finding arbutus and spring beauties. She left school to keep house, care for the one-year-old baby, Bernard, and help on the farm. She also took organ and sewing lessons. She planned to take boarders to add to the family income. Her first boarder was Bessie Lloyd, of Brockport. A warm friendship developed between Ella Morse and Bessie Lloyd, and when John Lloyd visited his sister he asked Ella to "keep company" with him. He wrote regularly to her every Tuesday evening. There was nothing in the letters which Ella could not have shown to everybody. Mr. Morse, however, disapproved of these attentions. He was afraid that his daughter would marry too early, leaving no one to care for the household and attend to the baby and sick mother. He soon began to intercept and destroy John's letters. Then John enclosed them in an outside envelope addressed them to Alfred the farmhand. Alfred put them in the hollow of a tree for Ella. When John asked Ella to marry him, her father forbade her to see him. John then planned an elopement. Ella left Addison at 5 A. M., May 5, 1878. John was waiting for her at Rochester. There they were married by the Baptist minister, who lived near the station. They then went directly to Brockport and were welcomed by John's father and sister. Ella wrote to her father for forgiveness, but she never heard one word from him. John and Ella remained in Brockport about one year, when John had a good position offered him in an iron factory in Syracuse. They stayed here less than a year and then moved to Rochester. Here John was, at various times, a butcher's assistant, a driver and an employee in an iron foundry. In 1883 Ella gave birth to a stillborn son. A daughter, Lula, was born on January 14, 1885, and in 1886 another daughter, Maude, was born. A son was born in 1887 and died the same year. John Lloyd ruptured an artery in his system in 1887. He was taken to a hospital. Two weeks later he died. Just before his death he had started a dry-goods store and had invested in it all his savings. Ella continued to keep the store; she took in sewing besides. Then her father-in-law came from Brockport to help her, but his presence proved a hindrance rather than a help. He wrote to Alexander Green, an acquaintance of John Lloyd's, to come and help them. Alexander Green entered Ella Lloyd's employ in 1889. Green spent his earnings on beer and had other bad habits. Ella knew this, but when a few years later he asked her to marry him, she consented. She wanted some one to protect her and her daughter, Lula. In 1892 they all moved to New York city. Alexander got a place as coal shoveler in a coalyard in West Forty-sixth street. His family lived for five years in a tenement house in the rear of the coalyard. In 1893 a son was born and died at birth. Another son was born the following year, dying a few weeks afterward. The family then moved to Eleventh avenue between Forty-fifth and Forty-sixth streets. A daughter, Elizabeth Rosanna, was born November 17, 1895. In 1897 the family moved to another tenement in the same street. Ella attributes her own ill-health and the death of her children to the dirty, damp and unhealthy house behind the coalyard. Another son was born and died in infancy in 1898. The family moved again to Eleventh avenue.

Lula Lloyd attended public school iregularly until her fourteenth year. Lizzie was sent to Public School No. 51 at five. Because of her ill-health she attends very irregularly. Lizzie is interested in a kitchen garden. She loves to draw also.

In 1892 Alexander worked at the coalyard at foot of Forty-sixth street for nine dollars a week. In 1897 he took to driving a beer wagon for twelve dollars a week. In 1903 he returned to his old work at ten dollars a week. He worked irregularly. He gave his wife only half his earnings. Frequently he demanded "beer money" besides. "To keep the wolf away" Ella took in sewing, chiefly children's dresses for the neighbors, and aprons at twenty-five cents a dozen. Often she acted as midwife for one dollar a day. Since 1900 she "has" taken in charge babies for eight and ten dollars a month. Since September, 1904, she has charge of three babies. Lula has been employed since 1899 successively as a candy packer, an employee in the Eagle Pencil Company, at a carpet factory. At present she works at a silk factory for five dollars a week.

Towards Lula, Alexander has always acted brutally. He insisted upon her paying board (one dollar weekly). In 1900 he drove her away. She lived with her uncle Bernard Morse in West Fourteenth street. To Lizzie, his own daughter, Alex "is alternately harsh and foolishly indulgent." He "gave her a piano teacher, fine clothes and expensive toys." Ella is inclined to be indulgent to both her children. She does not conceal from Lula her contempt for her husband. She speaks freely to her on all subjects. She does not insist upon truthfulness in regard to Lula's work hours. Delicate health gives one a tendency to shirk work, she says. Ella bought her a piano on the instalment plan. She encourages Lula to take piano and singing lessons. She wants Lizzie to be obedient, but the child usually has her own way. She has trained Lizzie to save her pennies and sell old clothes. Once Lizzie sold all the family footgear.

Ella attends the Janes Memorial Methodist Church, 461 West Forty-fourth street. Lula went to Sunday-school there. Since 1899, however, she goes with Mary Carpenter to the Episcopal Church. Lula "changed" because the Methodist service was "too dead slow." Ella does not encourage her church-going. "She might faint, it is so close, she is better off to home." Lizzie goes to the Methodist Sunday-school. On Saturday she goes to sewing-school to the Chapel of the Divine Providence. She thus gets "double Christmas presents."

Alexander has never been "stidy." He usually comes home "full and razes the roof off the house." He abuses Ella in the children's presence. Lula is the cause of the family troubles. He frequently overturns the supper table, breaks the dishes and throws the furniture at Ella's head. Often "he goes off on a tare." He threatens to desert her. Ella does not look forward to spending a green old age with him alone. In September, 1904, he "went off for good." "There were plenty of other women," he said. His kin "sides" with Ella. She is happier without him.

Alexander, Ella and Lula are insured in the Prudential Life

Insurance Company, at a premium of ten cents weekly. Lizzie pays five cents premium weekly to the same company.

Lula is keeping company with a neighbor. He takes her to "the racket" and she "gets presents off him." Ella knows nothing about Phil's family. He has a "good face and does not drink." She does not wish Lula to marry.

MONOGRAPH NO. XVIII. GEORGE ADAMS FAMILY. OBSERVED DECEMBER, 1903, TO MAY, 1904.

George Adams,	Age 40.	Blond; brown eyes; fair; inclined to excessive drinking habits.
Agnes Hebbel Adams,	Age 36.	Blond; gray eyes; fair; deaf; never ill.
George, Jr.,	Age 15.	Light brown hair; gray eyes; fair; liver trouble, 1900.
Albert, b. 1892. d. after six weeks.		Blond; gray eyes.
Child, Still-born, 1893.		
Charles, b. 1894. d. 1898.		Blond hair; gray eyes.
Christina, b. March, 1898.	Age 6.	Blond; gray eyes; fair; had scarlet fever and diphtheria, August, 1903.
Adam,	Age 2.	Blond; brown eyes; fair; scarlet fever and diphtheria, August, 1903.

George Adams was born in Tottenham, England, January 6, 1864. His mother died soon after his birth. He had nine brothers and sisters. He never told his wife their names or ages. His father was a blacksmith. He died of smallpox. The children attended a Protestant Sunday-school regularly. His wife never asked George about his schooling. "That is not important when you marry a man." Against the wishes of his brothers and sisters George came to New York at sixteen (1880). He came because he heard wages were higher here than abroad. He became an apprentice to a carpenter. He boarded with a family "down-town." "He never sent home for a cent and he never sent a cent home." He has no relatives in America.

Pierre Jacquot was born in Rouen, France, in 1818. Before he was ten he worked in a silk factory. He never went to school. In 1829 he was sent to America. His family stayed in France. He married a German Catholic in 1840. He spoke no German. His English was always broken. His wife spoke no French. The first child was born in 1841, a second in 1842. That year Pierre had to have all his teeth drawn. He claims that he lost the sight of one eye and became deaf through the carelessness of the dentist. Pierre had twelve children by his wife. The youngest of these was named Agnes, born about 1856. Then his wife died. The family lived in Buffalo and New York. Before the year was out he married again. By his second wife he had two children. Then they separated. Pierre kept the children of his first wife. (Agnes does not know just how many of them were alive then.) The second wife took her own children. He never heard of her again.

At sixteen Agnes married a German called Hebbel. Hebbel was born in 1831 and came to America about 1847. He was a laborer. Pierre Jacquot lived with the Hebbels. His other children married and went to New York city, New Jersey, Chicago, Milwaukee and Buffalo. The Hebbels had twelve children. Agnes, Jr., was born October 3, 1868, in West Twenty-seventh street. She remembers only eight brothers and sisters. Of these seven are living.

At three Agnes, Jr., had the measles. An aunt took her out into a snowstorm and ever since she has been deaf. At seven she attended public school in West Twenty-seventh street for three months. She did not like school, so she stayed away. No one at home cared whether she went or not. She was brought up a Catholic, but she never went to Sunday-school or church regularly. At nine she left home to get rich. She took a situation as a nurse girl for eight dollars a month with a family in West Eighty-second street. By 1880 she was working at her aunt's laundry. In 1881 she went to Milwaukee, on the invitation of her uncle, who was the owner of a mattress factory and employed one hundred men. Agnes went because she wanted "to get rich quick." She left her uncle's house after two months because her cousin thought "she was keeping company with her own feller." She took a position as a nurse. She lived with Jews. "They were a good deal like other folks." After a year her grandfather and her two aunts from Buffalo and New Jersey came out to see her. In 1883 she returned to New York. She became a laundress in a private family, for twenty dollars a month. The other servant was a colored girl. Agnes has liked "niggers" ever since. Agnes did odd jobs for her mistress and for them received extra pay. She cut off her long hair and sold it for twenty dollars to a lady who admired it. Her one ambition was to become rich. Before she married she said she had saved one thousand, one hundred dollars in the Franklin Savings Bank. In 1888 she "kept company," with a butcher, although she never had any use for men, theatres or "rackets." Money was much more to her taste. She had no desire to marry the butcher because he "might be mad and use the knife on me." At a surprise party, which was given at the house at which the butcher boarded, she met his friend, George Adams. Her mother met him, too, and "took a shine on him." On July 25, 1888, George visited Mrs. Hebbel and told her he wanted to marry Agnes. Afterwards he called on her where she was working. He told her he was tired of boarding. Agnes did "not see what he was after." He suggested a walk. They went to the Eden Musee. Then he spoke of boarding again and finally asked her to marry him. Agnes did not like him. He told her that her mother approved. Then she said she'd see. This was the understanding between them. The wedding day was set, although Agnes told her mother that she did not like George. George and the butcher made a bet of one dollar in her presence as to who would get her. She did not know her own mind, but the thought of the butcher flourishing his knife determined the question for her. George had to pay thirty-five dollars for the wedding. "I told him if I was not worth that he need not have me at all."

They were married August 2, 1888, in the "chapel" of the Catholic church as George was not a Catholic. Agnes wore a slate-colored dress and a white veil with roses. Her sister was bridesmaid. The rice and shoes were thrown at her sister, "so no wonder I had bad luck with my man." The wedding took place on Saturday. On Sunday her mother gave her a party. George wanted to go on a wedding trip, but Agnes did not "see the use of it." "Her feller had given her a grand time during the weeks of her engagement." George and Agnes went to live in Harlem. In 1889 George wanted to live down-town. They moved to Thirty-ninth street (1889-1890). The following year they moved to West Fifty-third street, and then in 1890 to Forty-fifth street, where they have lived ever since.

George, Jr., was born June 6, 1889. He was baptized in the Catholic church according to the agreement made by Agnes and George *before* their marriage. George, Jr., was nursed for over three years in spite of the fact that the neighbors said he would "turn out light-headed." Agnes said she had to nurse him that period of time because she had two miscarriages and an over supply of milk.

In 1892 Albert was born, and lived six weeks.

In 1893 a child was "born blue." Agnes said this was due to the fact that she swept the room a few hours before. She never provided for her children beforehand and never gave the doctor "long notice." She has had a neighborhood doctor "on and off" for the last twenty years. She dislikes having him when she is confined. She tells him lies "out of modesty" she says. She remains quiet only two days after her delivery. In 1894 Charles was born. The same day Agnes had gone to church. The priest made her give up her pew to a rich woman although he must have seen that "she was carrying a child." She felt so angry that she cursed the priest, the rich woman, and the church. "That was the end of my church going." This time she sent for the doctor, but it was too late. The delivery was "dead easy." She washed the baby herself. [Her mother lived in the same house, but she does not like "women meddling either."] Charles died in 1898 from spinal meningitis caused by a fall.

Christina or Annie was born in 1898. Then the doctor gave Agnes five dollars instead of charging for his services, because she was "such a brave woman." Annie was nursed two and a half years.

Adam was born December 28, 1902. He has been nursed fifteen months. "Whenever he cries or it is convenient to give it to him, during the night or day." He is not bathed during the winter. His hair has never been washed. All her children had "cradle caps." "If you want a child to be lucky you must not wash its hair for a year." Agnes "chased the Board of Health away" when they came to vaccinate him. "Should a child be vaccinated before it was five, it would kill it."

For a number of years George Adams has found employment at three "job carpenters." He earned about four dollars a day, but he rarely has work more than three days of the week. During the winter he is often unemployed. He belongs to the Brotherhood of Carpenters. His dues are seventy-five cents a month. If his wife dies first he is to receive fifty dollars and funeral expenses; if he dies Agnes is to receive one hundred dollars and funeral expenses. In case of sickness George is entitled to a doctor's services and five dollars a week "benefit." He has always refused to call in a physician because he thinks they "know nothing," and Agnes has always resented the entrance of a stranger, especially a man. George spends what he wishes of his wages and gives Agnes the "rest." Until about 1890 Agnes "washed out." She will have to work all her life because she washed for one of her mother's customers two days after her wedding. "All the neighbors prophesied this and it has come true." She has her own system of charging her customers. She asks more or less according to the "finery of the people." She used to earn "extra money" by telling fortunes from tea leaves for a "dollar a fortune." Agnes has shares in a building and loan association in Jersey, on which she pays eight dollars and fifty cents a month. She receives six per cent interest. This fact, as well as facts about her own earnings, she hides from her husband. She keeps her money in a stocking under the mattress until she takes it to the bank. She also at times keeps quarters in her shoes when she is not "going barefooted in the house." Since 1888 George has been insured in the Prudential Life Insurance Company, at a premium of twenty cents weekly, and in the Metropolitan at a premium of ten cents weekly. George, Jr., is also insured in this company, at a weekly premium of ten cents. Agnes and Annie are insured in the Hancock Life Insurance Company, at a weekly premium of ten and five cents, respectively.

George, Jr., has attended Public School No. 51 since 1896. He goes to Central Park with his teacher and he had a school garden plot at De Witt Clinton Park. He attended vacation school in 1901. In March, 1904, Annie went to the kindergarten in Public School No. 57. "Agnes never 'bothers' about going to the school." George takes his son to the Methodist Episcopal church in West Forty-fourth street occasionally.

George, Jr., and Annie go to Sunday-school at the Catholic church in West Forty-sixth street. George, Jr., says he likes the Methodist Episcopal church much better. Agnes only goes to church to "get churched." "It brings good luck." "Then mother and child must wear new clothes to please God." George, Jr., once smoked cigarettes. When I asked Agnes about it she said she could not stop him; she just "hits him on the mouth every time." She also swears at him and spanks him. He is not sparing in his language either because "Mama does not hear."

Agnes does not go to bed till twelve and one at night. She irons and sews the children's clothes at night. Sometimes she goes to see a friend. George never goes with her. Her friends never come at night because they dislike her husband. Saturday nights he goes to the saloon and comes home drunk. Each accuses the other of drinking. Agnes always has beer, sturgeon and biscuits at 10 P. M. Agnes always lies to George about her extra money, and she is always afraid of his finding her bank book. When he is out of work she does not like him at home, so she asks him to chop wood or carry water. That usually "sends him off." Agnes thinks it is much better not to marry and to have so many children. She says she likes her own, but thinks she would be better off if she had none. She does not know "why rich folks has so few and us poor ones so many." "If you are poor you ought to have only two." Should she die before George and he neglect the children she would "haunt him." After George and Agnes have had a quarrel she does not speak to him until he brings her a peace-offering.

MONOGRAPH NO. XIX. JAMES RAINEY FAMILY. OBSERVED FEBRUARY, 1904, TO MAY, 1904.

James Rainey,   Age 40.   Light brown hair; reddish-brown moustache; blue eyes; bloated face; frequently intoxicated; illiterate; irresponsible; rough.

Sarah Hannigan
  Rainey,   Age 38.   Blond; blue eyes; pale; freckled; pneumonia before confinement, 1895; superstitious; loquacious; suspicious.

Daughter,
  b. 1884.
  d. aged 7 months.

Sadie,   Age 19.   Blond; blue eyes; pale; freckled; undeveloped; narrow-chested; pneumonia at 10; diphtheria at 12; ignorant; given to lying; irresponsible; lazy.

Annie,   Age 15.   Blond; brown eyes; sickly; undeveloped; granulated eyelids; eyes operated on May, 1904.

James,   Age 14.   Brown hair and eyes; undeveloped; bright; truthful; friendly.

Katherine,   Age 13.   Brown hair; blue eyes; pale; emaciated; dull; untruthful; lazy.

Florence,
  b. 1892.
  d. "a few months old."

Daughter,
  d. at birth, 1893.

Daughter,
  b. 1895.
  d. aged two months.

Andrew,   Age 7.   Brown hair; blue eyes; pale; **measles, 1904**; bright; mischievous.

Robert, Age 16 months.   Brown hair and eyes; pale; thin; measles and sore eyes 1904.

James Rainey was born in Dublin, Ireland, about 1840. He married when he was about twenty. In 1862 he came to New York city. His wife had two sisters in Dublin. Her children never knew anything else about her family. In 1864 James, Jr., was born. The next year his mother had another son. Although this brother lives in New York, James has not seen him for years. James never knew whether there were any more children. In 1878 the family returned to Ireland and remained there for a year. James, Jr., does not remember what his father's work was or when his parents died. His wife would not "dare" to ask him. "He would think it queer." At fourteen James, Jr., went to work. His wife never asked him what he worked at before she married him. At seventeen he was "keeping company" with his present wife, Sarah Hannigan.

Sarah Hannigan was born in Monroe street, New York city, in 1866, in the school building of which her father was janitor (1863-1895). She never asked if her parents were native born and she knows nothing about her mother's family.

Sarah married James Rainey in 1883. They lived in Henry street until 1885. Within a year of the marriage a child was born. She died at the age of seven months. In 1885 Sadie was born, in 1889 Annie, in 1890 James, in 1891 Katie and in 1892 Florence. Florence was sickly and Sarah attributes this to her own ill-health before the child's birth. She lived only a few months. In 1893 another girl was born and she died at birth, unbaptized. In 1895 another girl was born and lived only two months. In 1897 Andrew was born. He was nursed the first month. After that he was given the bottle, besides "everything on the table." In 1902 Robert was born. He, too, is "a bottle baby." Besides that he is given hot biscuits, pork and beans, bananas, etc. And yet his mother does not understand why he has such a "weak" stomach. From 1883-1889 James was a letter carrier. In 1889 he was transferred to the Ninety-sixth street district. He cleaned the public school there in the evening. For this he received five dollars a week. In 1889 he became a conductor on the Forty-second street crosstown car lines. His wages would be eighteen dollars a week if it were not for the fact that he is usually drunk two days out of the week and unable to work. He gives his wife different amounts every week, twelve or fifteen dollars, as he spends more or less on whiskey.

The family lived in Henry street from 1883 to 1889. Then they moved to Ninety-sixth street and Third avenue for a year, and after that to West Forty-fifth street.

Sarah does little cleaning or washing. She says she is prevented from "tidying up because the children are 'round so much." I never saw her try to do so. The family live in two rooms. There is one bed in the bedroom. No bed linen is used. The children lie on straw or rags. Sarah avoids paying the rent as long a possible. Frequently she pawns some household article to do so. Once Sadie told me that her mother "hocked the weddin' ring her gentleman friend had given her."

Sarah is lazy and inefficient. She has worked since her thirteenth year very irregularly. Twice she has been at Higgins' Carpet Factory for a few months at a time, once at a hammock factory in West Forty-ninth street and for three months she worked at the American Biscuit Company. She was discharged for disorderly conduct and laziness. From April, 1903, to May, 1904, she was idle. In May, 1904, I procured a position for her at a bakery for five dollars a week. She had never earned more than three dollars and fifty cents before that. She has been "keeping company" since 1903. Her "gentleman friend" is apparently never at work. He "stops" with the Rainey's during the day. Sarah "does not mind him 'round." Although he and Sadie expect to be married soon, she has never asked him whether he can support her.

James and Sarah have no mutual interests except the children. James spends his "off hours" at the saloon. Sarah has not been outside of the house in years.[1] James never offered to take her anywhere. She has never told me that her husband is a drunkard. She says that he has a sore leg or that he has hurt his back, etc. She drinks "on the quiet" herself.

To the children the word papa suggests either some one who is "lying on the straw drunk" or some one who reproves them violently. Occasionally he has given them a few pennies for candy.

Sarah sends the children to school when they are seven, but their attendance is always irregular. Their mother has no idea of discipline beyond whipping them or speaking harshly to them "to make them mind." The children obey because they are

---
[1] Sarah and James both told me that the city was "bad enough without the country" when I suggested a visit to the Bronx.

"scairt of mama." They told me that "mama tells a pack of lies." The baby she makes a pet of.

MONOGRAPH NO. XX. CORNELIUS DESMORAN FAMILY. OBSERVED NOVEMBER, 1903, TO MAY, 1904.

Cornelius Desmoran,	Age 40.	White hair; blue eyes; bloated; complains of chronic cough and pain in chest, well-informed; pessimistic; antipathies; quick; vigorous; unwilling to work; called "honest Noll."
Mary Jane McGowan Desmoran,	Age 41.	Black hair and eyes; pale; emaciated; weak heart; "weak spells" since October, 1900; pleurisy, 1904; illiterate and bigoted; bad memory; makes inconsistent statements; sluggish; timid.
Cornelius, Jr.,[1]	Age 17.	Brown hair; blue eyes; bright; religious nature; eager to better his position; affectionate.
Therese,	Age 15.	Brown hair; blue eyes; pale; emaciated; undeveloped; complains of dizziness; has chronic headaches; granulated eyelids, 1903; dull; unambitious; morose; deceitful; given to lying; "simple"; did not know her own age; lazy.
Isabella,	Age 13.	Brown hair; blue eyes; pale; ill-fed; no eyelashes; granulated eyelids; wears spectacles; 1894, fell off chair; crippled and paralyzed on right side; wears brace; unable to walk; 1894-1900 "on and off" at the Hospital for Ruptured and Crippled, Lexington avenue and Forty-second street; optimistic; sensitive; given to telling untruth; deft in manual work; kind; shy.
Katherine,[2]	Age 12.	Brown hair; gray eyes; pale and emaciated; shy; quarrelsome; but has sunny disposition.
Daughter, b. 1893. d. after five months.		Convulsions.
Timothy,	Age 10.	Brown hair and eyes; pale; measles and scarlet fever, but mother does not remember date; untruthful; shy.

[1] Lives with his aunt. [2] Lives with her grandmother.

John,   Age 8.   Brown hair; blue eyes; fair; measles and scarlet fever.

Mary Jane, Jr.,[1] Age 6.   Light brown hair; blue eyes; stout; good color; well-nourished; never sick; truth-loving; affectionate; sunny disposition.

About 1860 Cornelius Desmoran and his wife came to New York city soon after their marriage. They had lived in the north of Ireland. From 1860 to 1868 they had six children, the oldest of whom died in infancy. Cornelius, Jr., was born in 1864. His father died in 1868, and his son does not know anything else about him. Cornelius's mother supported herself by going out to wash by the day. She left the children to shift for themselves. The mother went to the German church in West Thirtieth street, although she knew no German at all, because it was convenient. It was here that "Noll" had been baptized, but he never went to church much and became a "backslider." From seven to eleven he went to the parochial school in West Thirty-seventh street. At eleven "Noll" ran away from home. He became an iron builder and worked at his trade for twenty years. He was a "harum scarum" boy and saw little of his home. His mother died in 1887. Two years later his sister died and the home broke up. Cornelius knew nothing about his kinsfolk except that he heard his mother speak of an aunt and uncle. He says he is descended from the Earl of Des Moran. He "parted enemies" with his brother, so a sister, Kate, is the only relative he sees.

In 1885 Mary McGowan's brother John[2] introduced her to his "pal" Noll Desmoran. October 10, 1885, they were married at Holy Grace Church, West Forty-second street, although Noll insisted that he was not a Catholic. The first child, Cornelius, Jr., was born January 15, 1887. His mother nursed him during the night. During the day Noll's grandmother cared for him. On her death, his aunt Katie Desmoran took him to bring up. Therese was born in 1889. Her aunt Therese McGowan "stood for" her, at Sacred Heart. Mary Jane worked until the day before the child's birth. The baby was always sickly. Her parents call her "simple." They say it is the fault of the midwife. Mary Jane

---
1 Lives with her grandmother.   2 Monograph iii.

says that "Tessie" will never be any different. "Once sick, always sick." Isabelle was born March 28, 1894. She was left alone with Tessie when her mother went out. At four she fell from a chair and was paralyzed on the right side. "The child can not possibly grow up." "They all die you know." Belle spent six years in the Hospital for Ruptured and Crippled. Katherine was born in 1892. Aunt Katherine Desmoran "stood for her." Grandmother McGowan looked after the children during the day. About this time Cornelius absented himself from home for several weeks at a time. He was out of work, "drank hard and fell into bad ways." In 1894 a girl was born. Mary Jane had to work so hard that she could not nurse her. The child had "convulsions." Mary Jane did not think it necessary to call in the doctor. Then she died. For a while this sorrow kept Noll at home. He does not speak of her now without tears. In 1895 Timothy was born and in 1896 John. In 1898 Noll again left his wife. Mary Jane was too ill to work. She moved to her mother's with her children. After a few days Mary Jane, 3d, was born "with no father to look after her." The attending doctor charged ten dollars. John McGowan refused to pay it, but he "fed the children." Mary Jane McGowan "stood for" her grandchild at St. Raphael's Church, and has cared for her ever since 1900. In 1903 she also took Katie "to board and cheer her up." Cornelius came back in 1900. Until 1895 Cornelius had worked at the iron industry as a "bridge builder" or "in the shop and on the bench." He received two dollars and a half to three dollars and a half a day. In 1893 when work was slack he found employment with the Consolidated Gas Company. Gradually his work grew less. He received seven to eight dollars a week. "The Jews and Italians worked cheaper and displaced the older men." Then, too, his nervous energy was spent. He could no longer work on high buildings. Long weeks of lack of employment and hungry children "drove him to drink." He brought home less and less after 1895. Mary Jane went out as a charwoman for from seventy-five cents to a dollar and a quarter a day. Since 1902 she has been employed twice a week regularly at the Henrietta Industrial

School. Since her "weak spells" have increased she has grown despondent and has also taken to liquor, but she tries to work bravely.

The Desmorans move frequently. They are usually behind in their rent and they are often dispossessed. The following is a partial record of the places they have lived in:

1885-1887, West Fifty-ninth street and Tenth avenue; 1887-1889, West Forty-fourth street and Eleventh avenue; 1889-1891, West Nineteenth street; 1891-1892, West Twenty-eighth street; 1892-1895, they do not remember; 1895-1896, West Thirty-seventh street near Tenth avenue; 1896-1898, West Fifty-first street; 1898, 552 West Forty-fifth street. Since 1903 they have moved three times.

Cornelius, Jr., attended Saint Raphael's parochial school from seven to eleven. Then he went to work. In 1903 he was an office boy "down-town." He pays his aunt board. His parents never ask him about his wages. Sometimes he brings his mother a few dollars. Tessie was sent to Public School No. 51 at seven, then her mother thought it would be better for her to go to the parochial school; but she did not seem to get along with the Sisters, so she was sent back to public school. Her attendance at school is very irregular and she has failed of promotion several times. She earns twenty-five cents a week by "sitting with an old lady"[1] every day after school hours. Some times she washes the dishes at home. Bella did not go to school until she was nine. Then she was taken by a Penny Provident visitor to the Henrietta Industrial School in West Sixty-third street. In 1900 she went out to their country home. Katie has been attending the parochial school since she was seven years old. She earns pennies by running errands and begs her supper "off the neighbors." At their father's wish John and Timothy have been attending Public School No. 51 since they were seven.

Noll speaks of his oldest son with great pride. He says he can never forgive himself for having permitted his sister Katie to "take the boy," "but it is too late now to make him come back." He is gentle to crippled Bella and waits on her. He scolds the boys and calls them "good-for-nothing." Mary Jane is fond of

---
[1] Monograph iv.

her children, but she does not give them much attention. She never bathes them or washes their clothes. They have irregular hours for sleeping. Once I found them all asleep at noon. They had been up all night, as their father had not come home. Their mother pays more attention to sending them to Sunday-school than to week-day school. (They are sent to the "Sisters" on Saturday to say that they can not go to Sunday-school next day unless they have clothes. On Monday morning the new clothes are "hocked.") Mary Jane is especially proud of the fact that Cornelius, Jr., has been an altar boy at Saint Raphael's, where she herself goes if she has "clothes to wear," for four years. She is proud, too, of his hopes of some day becoming a priest. Mary Jane says "all married women are unhappy." "The children keep coming faster than you can get them shoes." (When the children do get shoes either she or Noll pawns them.) In the morning Noll frequently goes off to "find work." This means to lounge about in the corner saloon with his "pals." He tries to keep the knowledge of his drinking habits from his wife. She dreads his discovery that she too "hugs the bottle." Her father never had "much to do" with his son-in-law. He came to call when Noll was out. Her mother also stays away when he is around the house. She says that Mary Jane is abused and when Noll was ill she refused to see or help him. Even Mary Jane's brother, once a "pal" of Noll's, avoids him.

MONOGRAPH NO. XXI.   JOHN BADER FAMILY.   OBSERVED FEBRUARY, 1904, TO MAY, 1904.

John Bader,	Age 38.	Stubborn and knows his "own mind"; never reads; takes no interest in politics.
Annie Hoeck Bader,	Age 35.[1]	Brown hair; blue eyes; fair skin; sore leg (1903-1904) due to blood-poisoning; stolid; phlegmatic; stupid; distrustful, but friendly to those whom she knows; does not know whether husband is Republican or Democrat.
Eva,	Age 10.	Blond; blue eyes; pale; delicate; whooping cough, 1900; measles, 1902; fond of study; affectionate.

---
[1] She does not know whether this is correct.

Annie, Jr.,	Age 8.	Light brown hair; blue eyes; pale; measles, 1896; whooping cough, 1900; bashful; playful.
Harry,	Age 6.	Light yellow curly hair; blue eyes; ruddy; whooping cough, 1900; measles, 1902; friendly; lovable.
Frank,	Age 4.	Light yellow hair; blue eyes; pale; delicate; "weighed less than five pounds at birth"; "has always been sickly and given to taking cold"; does not speak easily; "spoiled."
William, b. August, 1904.		Blond; blue eyes; healthy.

John Bader was born in West Sixty-eighth street, New York city, in 1866. He was one of eight children. His father and mother were Germans. His wife does not know when they came to the United States. At seven he went to public school. At eleven he worked at a plumber's. Soon he gave that up and became a driver at a brewery, at Eleventh avenue and Forty-sixth street. In winter his wages are fifteen dollars weekly, in summer, when the working hours are reduced, only seven.

Annie Hoeck was born in 1869 on West Thirty-eighth street, New York city. Her father was a German, her mother an Englishwoman. They had twelve children, seven of whom are living. Her father had been employed in a sugar factory in Germany. He never had steady work in America, so he took his family abroad in 1872, in the hope of finding work there. After six months of failure in Germany and England, they returned to New York city. Annie went to school from 1876 to 1881. Her family attended the German Lutheran Church, where the services were held in German. Neither of her parents spoke English. From 1881 to 1893 Annie worked at a bakery in Grand street for twelve dollars a month. Her board and lodging were free. She slept behind the store with the other girls.

Annie does not remember how or where she first met John Bader. They were married April, 1893, in the German Lutheran Church in West Forty-second street, in spite of the objections of her parents to John as a Catholic. They moved to West Forty-fourth street. Eva, their first child, was born February,

1894. Annie says she knew all about babies from "seeing the young 'uns 'round her mother." In 1894 the family moved to West Forty-sixth street, near the river, where they have lived ever since. Annie says it is not "elegant" to move frequently. Annie, Jr., was born July 25, 1896, and Harry, November 23, 1898. Annie nursed them a long time, "so as to keep them from coming so fast." Frank was born in 1901. He was sickly from birth. Annie says that he will never be strong for that reason. He was christened in the Protestant Church, West Forty-second street. His maternal uncle "stood for" him. William, the youngest, was born in August, 1904. He was christened New Year's week at the Knox Memorial Church. He was named for his paternal grandfather. Annie had been saving her pennies in the Penny Provident Bank for several months previous to his birth.

John has not attended church since his marriage. He works Sunday mornings. For three years Annie has attended a Bible class at the Wilson Memorial Church (West Forty-second street), on Sunday evenings and goes to lectures there occasionally. She left the Lutheran Church because she thinks it "is foolish to have German services, and you get more Christmas presents there besides." Eva and Annie also attend the Sunday-school there.

Eva and Annie, Jr., were sent to Public School No. 17 at seven. Annie does not know in which class the children are. She keeps both of them home very frequently to help her, writing to their teachers that they have colds. Helping is more important than learning a lot "of things that do nobody no good anyway." She rarely sews or mends. The children either wear torn clothes or Annie buys new ones and discards the old ones. The children are taught to be "handy" 'round the house.

Annie says that her "man is good enough." He is easy-going and does not disturb her when he has "beer and tobacco." He pays eighty cents premium bi-weekly to the Hancock Life Insurance Company for the whole family. John never speaks of his parents to Annie or takes her to see them, although they live on Eleventh avenue between Forty-sixth and Forty-seventh streets, but he takes the children "over" occasionally on Sunday.

Then Annie goes to see her parents. She considers her father a model husband and father, "for he is sober and honest and does not chew, drink or smoke." Annie does not see her three brothers frequently, but two of her sisters come for "coffee" at least once a week and the third sister takes lunch with her daily.

MONOGRAPH NO. XXII. EMIL RAPP FAMILY. OBSERVED NOVEMBER, 1901, TO APRIL, 1902.

Emil Rapp,	Age 35.	Brown hair and eyes; fair; weak eyes, inherited from father; has improved in health since he gave up painting.
Gertrude Rapp,	Age 36.	Blond; blue eyes; fair; chronic headaches.
Josephine,	Age 12.	Blond; blue eyes; fair; thin and pale; takes cold easily.
Harry,	Age 10.	Blond; blue eyes; fair; weak eyes; headaches.

Charles,
  b. 1893.
  d. 1894.		

Theresa,	Age 4.	Blond; blue eyes; fair; weak eyes; bronchitis; chronic colds.
Emil, Jr.,	Age 2.	Blond; blue eyes; fair; pale; emaciated.

Emil Rapp, Jr., was born October 30, 1867. He was one of four children. His parents were both Germans by birth. The family lived in East Seventy-fourth street. Emil, Jr., was baptized in the German Catholic church of the neighborhood and later attended Sunday-school there. He went to public school until he was fourteen. (He is proud of his "education" and frequently takes books from the Free Circulating Library in West Forty-sixth street.) Then he helped his father in the fresco painting business. On Emil senior's death his sons, Emil and Harry, went into partnership together.

Gertrude Junge was born in West Thirty-eighth street in 1866. Her parents were also German by birth. They had thirteen children. Eight of these died in childhood. Gertrude's adult brother died in 1902 of blood poisoning. She sees very little of her sisters. They failed to come "round" when her last child was born, an unpardonable slight, and they never offered her "a red cent" when they knew she needed it. Gertrude went to Sunday-school at Holy Cross Church in 335 West Forty-second street. Her family were "church people." At eight she went to public school. She left because she was a "nervous child." Then she went to the Holy Cross parochial school for a few months and then to a private school in West Forty-second street. She now believes that the public schools are the best schools.

Gertrude met Emil Rapp in 1887. He told her that he had "lots of money put aside" and persuaded her to run away with him. They were married in February, 1887, by a Catholic priest. The disappointment "killed Gertrude's mother." Her father also died soon after her marriage.

Emil and Gertrude moved to rooms in West Forty-seventh street. Then Gertrude thought the district was not "swell enough," so in 1888 they moved to a flat in One Hundred and Fourth street and Madison avenue, where the rent was sixteen dollars a month. Emil's brother Harry and sister Josephine boarded with them. Josephine was born in 1890. Her aunt "stood for" her. Shortly before her birth the family moved to West Sixty-sixth street, where they lived two years at a rent of eight dollars and a half a month. Harry was born in 1892. His uncle "stood for" him. But in the same year Emil and Harry quarreled. Harry dissolved the partnership and moved away. Josephine also left the household. Emil has seen neither of them since then. In May, 1893, Charles was born. He died in September, 1894. At this time the family moved to West Forty-fifth street near Eleventh avenue. Theresa was born in September, 1898, and Emil, Jr., in 1900.

Emil did not "get along" as a fresco painter, although during the "busy season" he worked five days of the week for from three to three and half dollars a day. In 1902 he gave up his trade because he could not get jobs. He did not try to get work. "Everything is no use." Then he became an employé in the shop of the Hudson River Railroad, at Durham, N. J., at one dollar and forty cents a day. Gertrude tried to help out

by "washing out" two days of the week at fifty cents a day. Then "Jo" stays home to take care of the children. On Saturday afternoons Gertrude cleans an office for a dollar. When she is at home she keeps her rooms clean and neat, but she does not feed her family adequately. She thinks it economical to buy cheap food, and little at that. She prefers to spend the hard-earned quarter for Josephine's music lesson, and an hour of practice at Hartley House or the West Side Settlement. (She has planned for Harry "to play the fiddle.") The family is insured in the Hancock Life Insurance Company at a premium of forty-five cents a week.

Both children went to public school when they were seven. Josephine loves to study, and belongs to the library of St. Mary's Church. Gertrude intends to send her to high school and normal college. She is to be a teacher if she is "strong enough." Emil does not even want the children to go to Sunday-school, but Gertrude insists because "it keeps them off the streets and gives them good thoughts to carry home." She always dresses them in their "Sunday clothes." They go to Sunday-school twice on Sunday. They will "grow up good because they go so often." They also belong to a "church society at St. Mary's." Jo also goes to Friday afternoon sewing class and goes to Mass on Saturday morning. She was confirmed May 2, 1900. Harry sings in the choir. He receives twenty-five cents a month for this. He attends rehearsals on Wednesday and Friday evenings and Saturday morning. Then on Sunday he sings at High Mass.[1]

Until 1898 Gertrude was a good Catholic. Then she joined St. Mary's, a Protestant Episcopal church. She goes regularly to mid-week Mass, and is a member of the Woman's Guild.

Gertrude has never forgiven Emil for deceiving her about his money before their marriage. She has given up trying to arouse his energy in him. "It's all no use." She is glad that he does not "make her go fishing with him on Sundays like he used to when we was first married." "I used to hate it so." She is proud of the little landscapes in water color he has painted for her. On Easter, 1901, he gave her an azalea plant which she kept for

---

[1] This is considered a great privilege by the families. The child singer seems to have a special " Grace."

a long time. While she was at Sea Breeze in 1901[1] he cared for the plant, and surprised her by painting the kitchen floor and furniture.

In April, 1902, the family moved to New Jersey, because Emil has work there. Rents are cheaper there and Emil thinks it will be better for the children to grow up in the country.

MONOGRAPH NO. XXIII. FREDERICK MOLLER FAMILY. OBSERVED DECEMBER, 1903, TO MAY, 1904.

Frederick Moller, Age 33. Blond; blue eyes; clear, ruddy complexion; has never been sick; intelligent; interested in civic affairs; attends mass meetings and public lectures; thinks children ought to be brought up in country; says New York tenements are unhealthy; ambitious for his children; hopes boys will not be mere day laborers; courteous.

Margaret O'Keefe Moller, Age 34. Dark brown hair; blue eyes; flabby; freckled; strong; never ill; has "bad teeth"; gets up a few days after confinement, says she will die of tuberculosis because "it is in the family"; friendly, but reserved; is not superstitious; not imaginative; rather slow of comprehension; has given up reading; thinks care of children the first duty of a mother.

Frederick, Jr., Age 13. Light brown hair; blue eyes; ruddy color; strong and healthy; bright, eager student; mischievous.

Margaret, Jr., Age 9. Dark brown hair; brown eyes; dark skin; never sick; has had no children's illnesses; stupid; truthful; bashful.

Thomas, Age 7. Blond hair; blue eyes; fair; strong; no children's illness; bashful; unruly; quarrelsome.

John, Age 5. Blond hair; diphtheria, May, 1904; bright; friendly.

Edward, Age 4. Light yellow hair; blue eyes; fair.

Katherine, b. July, 1904.

---

[1] The family were receiving aid from the Association for Improving the Condition of the Poor in 1901 and got an invitation to Sea Breeze for two weeks.

Frederick Moller was born in West Thirtieth street, New York city, in 1871. His parents were Germans. He does not know when they came to New York. His mother's kinsfolk settled in Pennsylvania. His mother never spoke of her life prior to her marriage in 1868. Frederick never knew his father's trade. He thinks he was an only child. His father died in 1876. Then his mother supported herself by washing. He has no pictures of his parents.[1] Frederick went to public school in West Thirtieth street, from seven to thirteen. At thirteen he went to work in a piano factory "down-town" for three dollars and fifty cents a week.

Maggie O'Keefe, Frederick's playmate, was also born in West Thirtieth street in 1870. She knows nothing about her father's family. Her mother's maiden name was also "Irish sounding," but the family were "good Yankees" who lived in New Jersey. Her parents were married about 1850. In 1874 her father died of tuberculosis. A year later her mother died of the same disease. Maggie's only brother died at two of tuberculosis also. Maggie says "it's got hold of us and we can't escape it." After her mother's death she and two younger sisters lived with their oldest married sister. Maggie went to Public School No. 51 from five to thirteen. In spite of the fact that her children later attended the same school she has never entered the school building "since." From 1883-6 Maggie worked at Higgins' Carpet Factory for five dollars a week. She paid her board to her sister, but she did not like the treatment she received. Both Maggie and her sisters never saw this married sister "more than they had to" later on, which was once or twice a year. The other sisters see one another every week. In 1886 Maggie became a nurse-girl and later a chambermaid.

Frederick Moller came to visit Maggie on Sunday and Wednesday evenings. In 1891 they were married. Maggie had waited "so long" because she was a Catholic and Fred a Protestant. They agreed never to talk about their religious differences. The children were to be brought up "good Catholics." In 1893 Fred, Jr., was born. Maggie had felt sick beforehand,

---

[1] Frederick said there was "no sense in knowing about one's relations."

but she was "ashamed to consult a man" so she went to a "lady doctor." He was christened in the Catholic Church. Maggie cared for him just as she had for the "rich child." He was nursed seventeen months. In 1895 Maggie gave birth to a girl. This time she called in the doctor who had known her from childhood. In 1897 Thomas was born, in 1899 John, and in 1900 Edward. Maggie engaged a German midwife a few days before Edward's birth. Katherine was born July, 1904. She does not believe in "getting ready" beforehand. Maggie's rooms are usually cleaner than her neighbors. She washes the clothes once a week regularly. She never mends the clothes. She buys them "ready-made," and throws the torn ones away or sells them. Frederick Moller pays fifteen cents and Margaret and the children ten cents as a weekly premium to the Hancock Life Insurance Company and to the Prudential. The family has lived in the following places:

1891-2, 617 West Forty-sixth street; 1892-3, 606 West Forty-sixth street; 1893-4, 602 West Forty-sixth street; 1894-5, 608 West Forty-sixth street; 1897-9, East 171st street and Third avenue; East 140th street; 1899-1903, Tenth avenue and Forty-second street; April, 1903-September, 1903, Concord, N. H.; 1903, 457 West Forty-first street.

They moved to Harlem to be nearer Fred's work, and to Concord to find work, otherwise neither Fred nor Maggie could tell me why they had moved so frequently, except that in one case they "liked to get nearer the first floor." Fred expected to build a house on the "instalment plan" in New Jersey. He looked forward to having his own garden. He lost his job in New Jersey so the family returned to New York in 1905. They live in West Forty-fifth street near Tenth avenue.

Maggie is very proud of her husband. He does not even smoke or drink like the rest of them.

Maggie is regular in her care of the children. She bathes the older ones twice a week and the youngest daily. She would like to take them out for a daily walk, but she has no time, so Maggie, Jr., takes them out every afternoon. "When they get to the country they will be out all day," she said. Edward was nursed for two years. "The longer you keep up nursing them, the longer you are spared having another." Maggie says two children are enough for "poor folks." She was not at all anxious to have another baby. "Six children are too many for any woman, but you see I can't help myself." Maggie believes in "spanking." "It's the only way to make them obey." Nevertheless she "stuffs" them with cake and biscuits at all hours "to keep them quiet." Fred is interested in Fred, Jr.'s, progress at school. He helps him and Maggie, Jr., with their lessons and encourages Fred, Jr., to read. He bought him a three-volume American history for his birthday. He thinks that "girls need not know as much as boys," so he is not concerned about Maggie's progress. She has been "left back" several times. All the children go to school at five years of age. Fred believes "in leaving the younger children to the women," but he plays with them on Sundays. The children understand that they are not "to ask papa about church."

MONOGRAPH NO. XXIV. ISAAC SHAPIRO FAMILY. OBSERVED OCTOBER, 1901, TO MAY, 1902.

Isaac Shapiro, Age 30. Black hair and eyes; swarthy; sickly; epilepsy; malaria; lumbago; sprained ankle, 1902; energetic; "works when he is fit only for bed."

Marion Shapiro, Age 28. Brown hair; blue eyes; fair; diabetes since 1897; 1892 and 1897 miscarriages ("misses"); bright; not superstitious; provident; sympathetic.

Clarence Marion, "May," Age 14. Brown hair; blue eyes; fair; scarlet fever and diphtheria, 1903; bright; helpful.

Sarah Amelia, Age 4. Brown hair; blue eyes; fair.

Amelia Theresa White was born in 1845 in Sheffield, England. She was an only child. Her father owned a tobacco store. In 1865 Amelia married "young Thurlby," a soldier in the English army. The young people came to New York with Amelia's parents in 1865. The next year Amelia gave birth to a daughter,

Amelia, Jr., and a son. Then "the English wars broke out and the soldier returned to England and the regiment." He was never heard of again. John Gates was "a head esquire" in Sheffield, England, and was "quite well off." He married and had two children, a son and daughter. The children came to New York in 1864. Soon after the parents died. The daughter returned to Sheffield "to settle the estate." "She settled it all on herself" and her brother remained here.

He "kept company" with the "widder" Thurlby. They were married and took rooms in Morton street. Five children were born, three of whom died in infancy. The youngest was born in 1876. She was christened Marion Louise at St. Luke's Chapel, in Hudson street, where her mother was the "head pillar." Marion and her sister grew up with her half brother and sister. "They knew no difference for they all had the same mother." In 1880 Amelia's mother died and Amelia died a week later of "a broken heart." The father took care of the four children, "but he betted on the races and lost all his property." He was supported by his stepson, who works in a brewery. When he died in 1901 he "owned only the clothes on his back." His funeral expenses were paid for by means of the insurance his stepson had "kept up for him." The stepson married. The stepdaughter also married and left the family "for good and all." Marion Louise lived with her half brother's family. She went to public school. After school she had to care for the children, clean and run errands. She grew tired of hard work. She was eager to "be free and see more of life."

In 1889 Mr. and Mrs. Isaac Shapiro were living in Morton street. They had eight children. The youngest boy, Isaac, Jr., was born in 1874. Although the family were Orthodox Jews, Isaac, Jr., secretly joined the Episcopal Church (St. Luke's Chapel). His father heard of it and henceforth he was "lost to Israel."

Isaac and Marion were in the same class at school. They attended church together. In December, 1889, six months before their graduation they were secretly married by a Baptist minister. Each one returned home. They kept their marriage secret until after their graduation from school. Both "sides" were exceedingly angry. Marion's half brother, because she had married "a Jew, and an epileptic Jew at that." Isaac's father resented the fact that his son had not married "one of his own people."

In August, 1890, Isaac and Marion took rooms in Morton street. For the next few years "they lived up and down the street, and on most of the cross streets." They liked the Ninth Ward "because there is a better class of people down there." In 1891 the fifteen-year-old wife gave birth to a daughter. She was christened Clarence Marion at St. Luke's Chapel. Marion knew nothing about babies. Her married sister took "May" home and kept her for ten years. In February, 1900, the second child was born. She was christened Sarah Amelia for her father's sister and mother's mother. In 1901 the family moved to West Forty-fifth street, between Tenth and Eleventh avenues. Then Marion "took back May." May visits her "second mother" every week. In 1903 the family moved back to Leroy street, to their old ward.

Isaac started in business for himself three times. He failed every time, "not because of drink but hard luck." For five years he peddled potatoes for a wholesale dealer for about eight dollars a week. Then he worked as an expressman and still later as a fishman for nine dollars a week. In 1902 he went back to "his peddling." May went to Public School No. 51 until 1902. Marion sees that she attends school regularly and knows her lessons. She hopes May will be a teacher, "because the work is easy and there is nothing vulgar about it." May runs errands for her mother and "goes to the store" every day. Marion teaches the children to respect their father. Sarah brings him his slippers every evening.

Since 1901 the family have attended the Second Reformed Presbyterian Church in West Thirty-ninth street. Isaac has "left off going to church," but Marion attends at Christmas and Easter. She goes to mothers' meetings. She has received gifts of food and money from the church visitor. May is sent to Sunday-school there and she is a member of the Junior Christian Endeavor Society and the Loyal Legion.

Marion is fond of praising her husband. "You can only fall in love once—the real time. All the other times are something else." Isaac "turns over" all his wages to Marion. She in turn gives him "a quarter's spending money."

THE UNIVERSITY OF MICHIGAN

DATE DUE

DEC 3 1983

NOV 1 0

MAR 3 1984

MAR 1984

APR 1991

APR 3 0 1997

397

DO NOT REMOVE
OR
MUTILATE CARDS